REVISE BTEC TECH AWARD
Sport (2022)

REVISION GUIDE

Series Consultant: Harry Smith

Author: Jennifer Stafford-Brown

A note from the publisher

While the publishers have made every attempt to ensure that advice on the qualification and its assessment is accurate, the official specification and associated assessment guidance materials are the only authoritative source of information and should always be referred to for definitive guidance.

This qualification is reviewed on a regular basis and may be updated in the future.

Any such updates that affect the content of this Revision Guide will be outlined at

www.pearsonfe.co.uk/BTECchanges. The eBook version of this Revision Guide will also be updated to reflect the latest guidance as soon as possible.

For the full range of Pearson revision titles across KS2, KS3, GCSE, Functional Skills, AS/A Level and BTEC visit:
www.pearsonschools.co.uk/revise

Published by Pearson Education Limited, 80 Strand, London, WC2R ORL

www.pearsonschoolsandfecolleges.co.uk

Copies of official specifications for all Pearson qualifications may be found on the website: qualifications.pearson.com

Text and illustrations © Pearson Education Ltd 2022
Typeset and illustrated by PDQ Media
Cover image © Simple Line/Shutterstock

The right of Jennifer Stafford-Brown to be identified as author of this work has been asserted by her in accordance with the Copyright, Designs and Patents Act 1988.

First published 2022

25 24 23 22
10 9 8 7 6 5 4 3 2 1

British Library Cataloguing in Publication Data

A catalogue record for this book is available from the British Library

ISBN 978 1 292 43614 2

Printed in Slovakia by Neografia

Acknowledgements

TEXT:

P22: Harper Collins Publishers Limited: BIZLEY, K. et al. (2010) BTEC First Sport Level 2, London: Harper Collins Publishers Limited p. 303

P22: Topend Sports: Robert Wood, "Cooper Fitness Test Norms." Topend Sports Website, 2012, https://www.topendsports.com/testing/norms/cooper-12minute.htm, Accessed 20 June 2022

P23: Topend Sports: Robert Wood, "push-up test: Home fitness tests." Topend Sports Website, 2008, https://www.topendsports.com/testing/tests/home-pushup.htm, Accessed 20 June 2022 (2)

P22: Rowman & Littlefield Publishing Group, Inc.: Cooper, K. H. 1982. The Aerobics Program for Total Well-Being. New York: M. Evans and Company, Inc. (2)

P24: YMCA of the USA: Sinning, Wayne E., Golding, Lawrence Arthur., Myers, Clayton R. Y's Way to Physical Fitness: The Complete Guide to Fitness Testing and Instruction. United States: YMCA of the USA, 1989.

P25: Topend Sports: Robert Wood, "Plank Core Strength and Stability Test." Topend Sports Website, January 2016, https://www.topendsports.com/testing/tests/plank.htm, Accessed 10 June 2022

P26, P30, P41: Harcourt Publishers: DAVIS, B. et al. (2000) Physical Education and the Study of Sport, 4th ed. London: Harcourt Publishers. P129, P123 (3)

P31: Wolters Kluwer Health, Inc.: McARDLE, W. et al. (2000) Essentials of Exercise Physiology. 2nd ed. Philadelphia: Lippincott Williams & Wilkins p. 394

P32: The Department of Health and Social Care: Contains public sector information licensed under the Open Government Licence v3.0

P33: The American Council on Exercise: © The American Council on Exercise

P34: Topend Sports: Han, T & Leer, E & Seidell, Jaap & Lean, M. (1995). Waist circumference action levels in the identification of cardiovascular risk factors: prevalence study in a random sample. BMJ (Clinical research ed.). 311. 1401-5. 10.1136/bmj.311.7017.1401.

P35: Harcourt Publishers: Davis, B. et al. (2000) Physical fitness and fitness testing, In Davis, B. et al. Physical Education and the Study of Sport. 4th ed. London: Harcourt Publishers. p. 129

P36: Topend Sports: Robert Wood, "T-Test of Agility." Topend Sports Website, 2008, https://www.topendsports.com/testing/tests/t-test.htm, Accessed 16 June 2022

P37: Topend Sports: Robert Wood, "Stork Balance Stand Test." Topend Sports Website, 2008, https://www.topendsports.com/testing/tests/balance-stork.htm, Accessed 29 June 2022

P44: BrianMac Sports Coach: MACKENZIE, B. (2004) Ruler Drop Test [WWW] Available from: https://www.brianmac.co.uk/rulerdrop.htm [Accessed 29/6/2022]

PHOTO:

123RF: Nicolas Fernandez 25, 67 (2), Aleksandr Davydov 54, lightwise 59br; Alamy Stock Photo: Rupert Rivett 7bl, Alys Tomlinson/Cultura Creative RF 64; Getty Images: FatCamera/E+ 5, FlamingoImages/iStock/Getty Images Plus 6, Avid_creative/E+ 6, FADEL SENNA/AFP 12, Lighthousebay/iStock/Getty Images Plus 12, BanksPhotos/E+ 30, FatCamera/E+ 51, SolStock/E+ 62; Pearson Education Ltd: PDQ Digital Media Solutions Ltd 24, 26 (2), Oxford Designers & Illustrators Ltd 58tr; Shutterstock: Sirtravelalot 1, Mangpor2004 2, Logoboom 3, BearFotos 9, Syda Productions 10, Photobac 10, Kameel4u 11, Nicole Weiss 14tr, Koya979 14cr, ArtRoms 14br, Galina Barskaya 15, Billion Photos 17tc, Burnel1 17tr, art3 28, Sirtravelalot 32, Microgen 44, Bobex-73 46, Blend Images 48, Syda Productions 50, Sahara Prince 54, 1185467 56, Galina Barskaya 57, Nejron Photo 57, Dmitry Rukhlenko 58cr, Flashon Studio 58br, Cameron Whitman 59tr, Alila Medical Media 59cr, Maanas 61.

Notes from the publisher

1. While the publishers have made every attempt to ensure that advice on the qualification and its assessment is accurate, the official specification and associated assessment guidance materials are the only authoritative source of information and should always be referred to for definitive guidance.

Pearson examiners have not contributed to any sections in this resource relevant to examination papers for which they have responsibility.

2. Pearson has robust editorial processes, including answer and fact checks, to ensure the accuracy of the content in this publication, and every effort is made to ensure this publication is free of errors. We are, however, only human, and occasionally errors do occur. Pearson is not liable for any misunderstandings that arise as a result of errors in this publication, but it is our priority to ensure that the content is accurate. If you spot an error, please do contact us at resourcescorrections@pearson.com so we can make sure it is corrected.

Websites

Pearson Education Limited is not responsible for the content of any external internet sites. It is essential for tutors to preview each website before using it in class so as to ensure that the URL is still accurate, relevant and appropriate. We suggest that tutors bookmark useful websites and consider enabling students to access them through the school/college intranet.

Introduction

Revising Component 3 of your BTEC Tech Award in Sport

This Revision Guide has been designed to support you in preparing for the externally assessed component of your course.

The assessment for Component 3, Developing Fitness to Improve Other Participants Performance in Sport and Physical Actvity, is in the form of a paper comprising short, long and extended writing questions. This will be completed under supervised conditions in a specified time. This assessment is likely to take place towards the end of your course. You will be expected to link knowledge and understanding with the other components.

Your revision guide

Each unit in this Revision Guide contains two types of pages, shown below.

Content **pages** help you revise the essential content you need to know for Component 3.

Skills **pages** help you prepare for your assessment.

Skills pages have a coloured edge and are shaded in the table of contents.

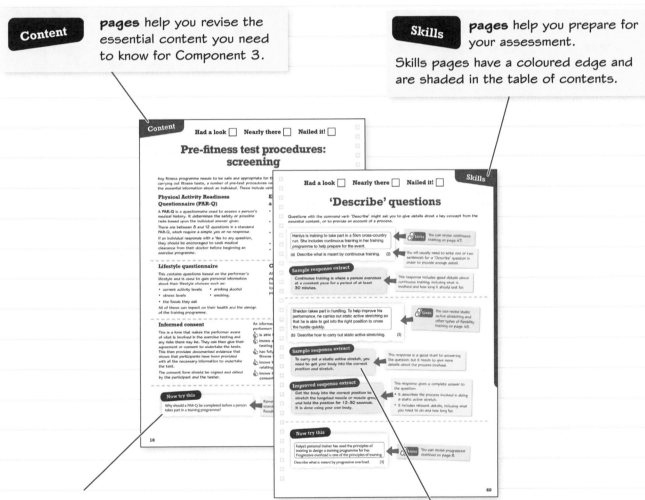

Use the **Now try this** activities on every page to help you test your knowledge and practise the relevant skills.

Look out for the **sample response extracts** to example assessment tasks on the skills pages. Post-its will explain their strengths and weaknesses.

Contents

A small bit of small print
Pearson publishes Sample Assessment Material and the Specification on its website. This is the official content and this book should be used in conjunction with it. The questions in Now try this have been written to help you test your knowledge and skills. Remember: the real assessment may not look like this.

The importance of fitness for successful participation in sport

There are a number of different components of fitness. These are grouped into components of **physical fitness** and components of **skill-related fitness**. Many sports will require high levels of one or more specific components of fitness in order to perform well in that sport.

Components of physical fitness

- **Aerobic endurance**: required for the cardiovascular system to keep supplying oxygen and nutrients to the body during events or sports lasting more 30 minutes such as long-distance running.
- **Muscular endurance**: required for the muscles to be able to keep contracting for sports lasting more than 30 minutes such as cycling.
- **Muscular strength:** required for sports and events that require high levels of force such as throwing a shotput.

- **Speed**: required for sports or events requiring fast movement such as 100 m sprint.
- **Flexibility**: required for activities needing a wide range of movement around a joint such as gymnastics or martial arts.
- **Body composition**: particular types of body composition can be required to perform well in certain sports such as gymnastics requiring low body fat or rugby players having a high muscle mass.

Components of skill-related fitness

- **Power**: required for explosive movement such as vaulting in gymnastics or performing a lay up in basketball.
- **Agility**: required for activities that need quick changes of direction such as dodging the opposition in a team game or in freestyle skiing.
- **Reaction time**: required for any activity where a quick decision or response to a stimulus is needed such as a swimmer diving into the pool to start a race.

- **Balance**: required for an activity where the person needs to control the distribution of their weight or to remain upright and steady such as a gymnast on a balance beam.
- **Coordination**: required for any activity where the person is having to move two or more body parts and can include the use of sporting equipment. For example, in tennis, the hand, eyes and tennis racquet all need to be coordinated to allow the person to connect with the tennis ball.

Team sports

In many team sports, specific players will require high levels of different components of fitness to play well in their position.

In football, a goalkeeper will need high levels of power to be able to jump up high to reach an overhead shot on goal, high levels of flexibility when diving to save a ball, agility when changing direction to save a deflected shot and fast reaction times to respond quickly to a penalty shot.

Now try this

Sheldon takes part in open-water long-distance swimming events that take one hour or longer to complete.

Sheldon will need to keep supplying his body with oxygen and nutrients and keep his arm and leg muscles contracting to propel him through the water for longer. Think about which components of fitness are required for sports that last longer than 30 minutes.

1 Which **two** components of fitness will Sheldon require to do well in open-water long-distance swimming?

a) Speed and balance

b) Power and coordination

c) Muscular endurance and aerobic endurance

d) Muscular strength and agility

Had a look ☐   **Nearly there** ☐   **Nailed it!** ☐

The basic principles of training: FITT principles

The letters of FITT stand for the key principles to follow when planning a training programme.

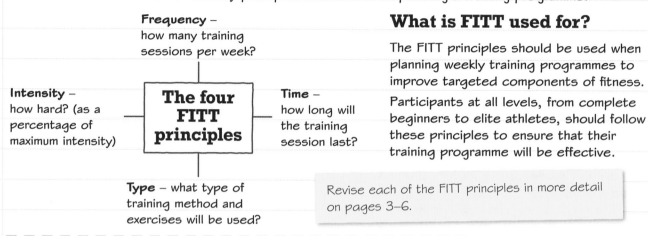

Frequency – how many training sessions per week?

Intensity – how hard? (as a percentage of maximum intensity)

The four FITT principles

Time – how long will the training session last?

Type – what type of training method and exercises will be used?

What is FITT used for?

The FITT principles should be used when planning weekly training programmes to improve targeted components of fitness.

Participants at all levels, from complete beginners to elite athletes, should follow these principles to ensure that their training programme will be effective.

Revise each of the FITT principles in more detail on pages 3–6.

Applying the FITT principles

Day	Training
Mon	30 minutes continuous training Jogging – 60% max heart rate
Tue	Rest day
Wed	30 minutes continuous training Jogging – 60% max heart rate
Thu	Rest day
Fri	30 minutes continuous training Jogging – 60% max heart rate
Sat	60 minutes continuous training Cycling – 60% max heart rate
Sun	60 minutes flexibility training (static stretching) Yoga class – moderate intensity

Frequency has been applied – there are five training sessions this week.

Intensity for jogging and cycling is given as percentage of maximum heart rate.

Time is given – each training session lasts between 30 and 60 minutes.

Type of training is given (continuous, flexibility) and type of exercise (jogging, cycling, static stretching).

The table shows an example of a training programme for a 60-year-old male where the FITT principles have been applied.

You can revise maximum heart rate on page 4.

Make sure that the **type** of exercise chosen will help the participant achieve their goals. Yoga is a popular activity for developing flexibility.

Now try this

The FITT principles are used to plan training programmes.
1 Identify what the letters F and I stand for in the FITT principles.
2 Give an example of how you can apply each of these principles in a weekly training programme.

Frequency

In the FITT principles, frequency means the number of training sessions completed every week.

Deciding frequency

When deciding on the frequency of training sessions you need to strike a balance between:

- providing sufficient stress for adaptations in the body to occur
- allowing enough rest periods for the body to heal and repair from the exercise sessions.

Progression and overload

You must take progression and overload into account when planning the frequency of sessions in a training programme.

There should be a gradual increase in stress placed upon the body, combined with a gradual increase in the frequency of training sessions.

Revise progressive overload on page 8.

 Real world **Example: Beginner's training programme**

Beginners should start with about three training sessions per week, and build up to more sessions per week as their bodies adapt to the training.

Week	1	2	3	4	5	6
Frequency of training sessions	3	3	4	4	4	5

This training programme provides a gradual increase in the number of training sessions each week.

Why increase the frequency of training sessions?

1 Participant takes part in a training session → **2** Increased level of fitness due to **adaptation** to training → **3** The participant can train more frequently → **4** Further increases in the participant's level of fitness

Adaptations are the body's responses to training that make it more able to cope with the stresses of the exercise. For example, muscle tissue adapts to strength training by getting bigger.

Frequency for training specific components of fitness

- **Muscular strength/muscular endurance** – two to three sessions per week.
- **Flexibility** – should be incorporated into the warm-up and cool down of every exercise session.
- **Speed and power** – frequency will depend on the specific sport, but two to three sessions a week are usually appropriate.
- **Aerobic endurance** – the weekly training programme should include a minimum of three sessions that target aerobic endurance, such as fartlek training.

Running up sand dunes and jogging back down is an example of fartlek training.

Now try this

Adam is training for a 10 km road race.

1 Identify the minimum number of weekly training sessions Adam should complete to improve his aerobic endurance.

Jess is a 400 m hurdler and trains four times a week.

2 Identify how many times Jess should take part in flexibility training.

Intensity

Intensity means how hard a person is exercising or how much effort they are putting into the exercise.

Determining intensity

It is important to train at the right intensity to target the chosen component of fitness and lead to adaptations.

The level of intensity can be altered by changing factors in the training session such as:

- increasing or decreasing the weight used (resistance) in strength training
- covering a longer or shorter distance in aerobic endurance training
- spending more or less time exercising.

Measuring intensity

There are two ways to measure intensity:

 Borg Rating of Perceived Exhaustion

If a person does not have a heart rate monitor to measure their heart rate, they can use the Borg Rating of Perceived Exertion (RPE). The RPE scale ranges from 6 (rest) to 20 (exhaustion). The person exercising indicates the number that represents how hard they feel they are working.

Score	Perceived exertion
6	No exertion
7–8	Extremely light
9–10	Very light
11–12	Light
13–14	Somewhat hard
15–16	Hard
17–18	Very hard
19	Extremely hard
20	Maximum exertion

Multiply the score by 10 to get an estimate of the person's heart rate (in beats per minute) during the workout: RPE × 10 = HR (bpm)

 Percentage of maximum heart rate (Max HR)

For some types of activity, working at the right intensity means a person exercising so that their heart is beating at a percentage of their Max HR.

Use the formula: Max HR = 220 – age

> **Real world Example**
>
> Zoya is 15 years old. She wants to work at 70 % of her Max HR to train her aerobic endurance.
>
> **Step 1** Calculate Zoya's Max HR:
>
> Max HR = 220 – 15 = 205 bpm
>
> **Step 2** Then work out 70 per cent of her Max HR:
>
> 205 × 70/100 = 144 bpm

Measuring HR

Pulse points: you can measure HR at pulse points. The radial pulse on the wrist and the carotid pulse in the neck are good places to measure HR. Count the number of heart beats for 30 seconds, and multiply by 2.

Technology: there are lots of technological devices that can be used to measure HR, including smart watches, apps and HR monitors (see page 14).

One Rep max for strength

One rep max is the maximum amount of weight a person can lift in one go. It is used to work out the load a person should lift when they are training to increase strength.

This can be used as a measure of intensity. For example, if a participant's one rep max is 100 kg, they can work out the weight they should lift to train at 80% intensity.

80/100 = 0.80

0.80 × 100 = 80 kg

To develop strength, heavy loads (above 70% intensity) are used and low reps.

15 rep max for muscular endurance

15 rep max is the maximum amount of weight a person can lift for 15 repetitions. To develop muscular endurance, low loads (below 70% one rep max) and high reps are used.

Now try this

Susie is 18 years old and takes part in continuous training. She wants to work at an intensity of 70–80 % Max HR, to train aerobic endurance.

 Round your answer to the nearest whole number (bpm).

1 Calculate Susie's Max HR.   **2** Calculate 70% of her Max HR.

Type

Make sure that the type of training you choose targets a specific component of fitness. You will need to consider both the type of exercise the person will take part in and the training method.

Which training type?

The type of training selected for a training programme should be determined by:

- the sport or activity the person takes part in
- the component of fitness the person wants to develop.

 Example

A shot-put thrower wants to improve their strength. An appropriate activity would be free weight training, targeting the main muscles used to throw the shot put.

Selecting the type of exercise and training method

Component of fitness	Types of exercise (examples)	Training methods (examples)
Aerobic endurance	Running, cycling, swimming, rowing	Continuous training, fartlek training, interval training
Muscular endurance	Body weight exercises – tricep dips, press-ups, lunges, squats, sit-ups	Circuit training
Strength	Free weights – bicep curls, bench press, knee extensions, hamstring curls, shoulder press	Resistance machines, free weights
Flexibility	Standing stretches, lying down stretches, using a partner or object to stretch	Static stretching, dynamic stretching, PNF stretching
Power	Lunging, jumping, hopping, sprinting uphill, using different equipment to develop power in upper and lower body	Plyometrics, anaerobic hill sprints, CrossFit
Speed	Sprinting on a running track, using sport-specific speed and agility equipment	Interval training, sprint training, SAQ
Agility	Ladders, dodging opponents	SAQ training
Balance	Standing on one leg, using a wobble board	Balance training
Coordination	Catching a ball, dance movements	Coordination training
Reaction time	Sprint start, football penalty kick goal saves	Reaction time

Variety of training methods

It is important to vary the training methods to avoid boredom.

For example, a person who wants to develop their aerobic endurance so that they can run 5 km should carry out running-specific training, but use different types of training in different environments. Appropriate training activities could include:

- jogging on a treadmill or using a cross-trainer
- cross-country jogging
- jogging round an athletics track
- jogging with a group of people in a running club.

Running with a group can help to prevent boredom. Park Runs cover a distance of 5 km, they are free and staffed by volunteers.

Now try this

Tanya is a gymnast. She wants to improve her power so that she can jump higher when performing her floor routine.

Describe a type of exercise that Tanya could carry out to improve her power.

Time

The length of time spent in a training session should be enough to encourage progressive overload. It should also be appropriate to the type of training and the component of fitness being trained.

High-intensity interval training (HIIT), cardiovascular and fat-burning activities

How long you should spend in a training session for these activities will depend on the component of fitness being developed and the purpose of the training.

* HIIT for developing aerobic and anaerobic fitness – short duration (30 seconds to 1 minute), with rest periods no longer than 30 seconds. Training sessions usually last up to 30 minutes.
* Cardiovascular activities for developing aerobic endurance – at least 20 minutes.
* Fat-burning activities use body fat as a fuel so are good for people who want to lose excess body fat – at least 28 minutes.

You can revise the different training zones on page 13.

Strength and muscular endurance activities

Strength and endurance training timeframes are based on the number of sets and reps for each muscle group. The participant must train for the time it takes to complete the required number of sets.

* The number of reps is how many times the exercise is repeated.
* The number of sets is how many lots of reps the participant completes.

For example, to develop muscular endurance of the biceps, the training could be: bicep curls – three sets of 15 reps.

Strength training requires a:
* low number of sets
* low number of reps
* high load/heavy weights.

Muscular endurance training requires a:
* high number of sets
* high number of reps
* low load/light weights.

Now try this

Sean is 28 years old and is trying to lose excess body fat.

1 Identify **one** type of exercise Sean could take part in to help him lose body fat.

2 State the minimum length of time Sean should take part in the exercise in order to lose excess body fat.

* Select exercises that Sean can keep performing for at least the minimum amount of time.
* Activities that are used to develop aerobic endurance or muscular endurance will be appropriate here.

Had a look ☐   Nearly there ☐   Nailed it! ☐

Additional principles of training: specificity

As well as the FITT principles, there are six additional principles of training that you can use to plan a training programme. Using these principles will help improve a participant's physical fitness and sporting performance.

Specificity
Training for specific components of fitness

Reversibility
Effects of stopping training.
Revise this on page 11

Adaptation
Changes to the body.
Revise this on page 10

The principles of training

Rest and recovery
Time where a participant does not take part in physical activity.
Revise this on page 10

Progressive overload
Gradually increasing workload.
Revise this on page 8

Individual differences
Taking into account current levels of fitness and sport.
Revise this on page 9

Variation
Changes in training programme routine.
Revise this on page 12

What is specificity?

Specificity means choosing a training method that develops a specific component of fitness which benefits participation in a particular sport or activity.

The remaining six principles of training can then be applied to this specific training method.

Applying the principle of specificity

To apply the principle of specificity, you need to make sure that the training methods are matched to the demands of the sport or activity that the participant is training for. For example:

- A netball player could take part in circuit training to develop muscular endurance. The stations would focus on upper body and lower body muscular endurance, as the arms and legs are used to play netball. Some circuit stations could include netball-specific drills such as passing and dodging.

- A long-distance cyclist could take part in road cycling to develop aerobic endurance. They could also train at home on their bike using a turbo trainer, use a stationary bike in a gym and take part in spin classes.

A turbo trainer is a device for cycling training. It allows you to pedal a normal bicycle but without travelling anywhere.

Now try this

Ryan is a rower. He is going to take part in a race in six weeks' time, and wants to improve his fitness for the event.

Describe **two** ways in which Ryan could use the principle of specificity to improve his rowing performance.

Progressive overload

Progressive overload means gradually increasing the participant's workload over time.

Applying the principle of progressive overload

Fitness can only be improved by **overloading** – training at a higher level than you normally do. Working harder in exercise sessions stimulates your body to adapt to the training. This will improve your fitness levels in the component of fitness being trained.

- If you do not overload, your fitness will not improve beyond its current levels.
- Overload is achieved by increasing the frequency, intensity and/or length of time spent training.
- Overloading should be **progressive** – the training programme should provide a gradual increase in the frequency, intensity or time spent exercising. This is necessary to avoid injury and overtraining.

Revise overtraining on page 11.

Progressive overload using time

A person who is training to take part in a long-distance race might undertake continuous training to improve their aerobic endurance.

- To apply progressive overload in this situation, gradually increase the **time** the participant spends training.
- As the length of the training sessions increases, the distance the participant runs will naturally also increase over the course of the training programme.
- For example, they can run further in a 50-minute session than in a 30-minute session.

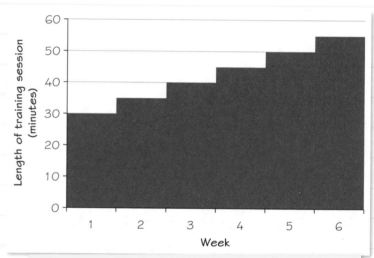

Start with a short training time and gradually increase.

Progressive overload using percentage of maximum heart rate (Max HR)

You can apply progressive overload to a training programme by increasing the **intensity** at which the participant exercises, using percentage of Max HR.

- In interval training, the training sessions could be planned so that each week the percentage of the participant's Max HR is increased to a slightly higher level during exercise periods.
- Once the desired maximum intensity has been achieved, increase the time spent exercising at the higher intensity in order to maintain progressive overload.

Progressive overload in strength training

To train for **strength**, the weights or resistance used should progressively increase. The participant's muscles will continually have to adapt to meet the demands of lifting increasingly heavier weights.

Week 1   Week 2   Week 3   Week 4   Week 5   Week 6

The overload can be achieved by keeping the number of reps and sets the same, but increasing the weight lifted.

Now try this

Give a definition of progressive overload.

Individual differences

For a training programme to be effective, the training should meet the needs of the individual. These will be different for each person.

Factors to consider for individual differences

Age – a younger person may require more games-based training compared to an older teenager or adult.

Sporting experience – a beginner in a sport will require a very different type of training programme compared to an elite sportsperson.

Current levels of fitness – a person with high levels of fitness is able to train more frequently and at a higher intensity compared to a person with low levels of fitness.

> **Each factor should be taken into account when planning a training programme for an individual.**

Low impact – where one foot is always in contact with the ground in the activity such as in walking.

High impact – both feet are off the ground at some point in the activity such as in running.

Sex – the sex of a person can have an impact on the type and intensity of training and recovery time frames due to the different hormone levels associated with the different sexes.

Weight – the weight of a person may impact on the type of training they can safely take part in, for example, if an individual has high body fat composition, then low impact training methods may be more appropriate to reduce the stress on their joints that could occur from high impact training.

Training methods

The training methods selected must be appropriate to train the identified components of fitness.

The types of exercise used for each training method should be sport-specific.

Revise the principle of specificity on page 7.

Individual lifestyle

It is important that the training is accessible to the individual. They must be able to:

- get to the location of the training
- afford to take part in the training
- fit the training around other commitments such as work or homework and family commitments.

Meeting an individual's needs

To meet the individual's needs, the training programme should be:

- appropriate for their sport or activity
- appropriate for their fitness levels
- chosen to suit their likes and dislikes
- accessible – the equipment and facilities must be accessible, available and affordable
- varied, to avoid boredom and to work a range of body areas and/or components of fitness.

On page 60, you can revise gathering information to devise a personalised training programme.

The cost of taking part in training might include the cost of any special clothing, footwear and equipment required, as well as the hire of facilities, gym membership or class fees.

Now try this

Jackie is a 15-year-old student and plays tennis. Her nearest tennis court is 5 miles away.

Describe **three** individual factors related to Jackie's lifestyle that may affect her accessibility to training.

This question is focused on accessibility to training, which is related to how she can get to the training, the cost of training and commitments she may have that could impact on her availability to train.

Rest and recovery and adaptation

Rest and recovery and **adaptation** are two additional principles of training, and both are required so that a person's fitness levels can increase.

Rest and recovery

Rest and recovery is the process of having time where a person does not take part in any physical activity. This principle must be followed to allow the body to recover and adapt to the training that the person has undertaken.

Most training programmes should have at least one rest day a week.

Adaptation takes place during the time given for rest and recovery.

Nutrition

Appropriate nutritional intake should be included in a training programme to support the recovery process. For example, if a person is trying to increase their muscular strength they should consume foods high in protein to support muscular repair and growth process.

Adaptation

An adaptation is a response of the body to training that makes it more able to withstand the stresses of the training.

Types of adaptations include:

*   an increase in muscle size from strength training
*   an increase in capillaries around muscle tissue from muscular endurance training.

These adaptations allow a participant to improve the component of fitness that is being trained.

However, these improvements are reversible. If training stops, the body will eventually return to its pre-exercise state.

This could mean reduced muscle size or a reduced number of capillaries around muscle tissue.

Examples of adaptation to training

Increase in muscle size from weight training.

These adaptations are **reversible**. If training stops, the body will eventually return to its pre-exercise state, such as a reduction in muscle size (see page 11 for more on reversibility).

Increased range of movement around a joint from flexibility training.

Points to remember

✓ Training programmes should include at least one rest day per week.

✓ Adaptation takes place when a person is resting and recovering from training.

✓ Appropriate nutrition is important to help with muscle repair and to replenish the body's energy stores.

✓ If appropriate rest and recovery is not included in a training programme it can lead to **overtraining** (see page 11).

Now try this

Describe why it is important to include at least one rest day per week in a training programme.

Reversibility

Reversibility means that the fitness gains that have been made from previous training start to decline, and a person starts to lose their fitness levels. Reversibility can be summed up by the phrase, 'Use it or lose it'.

Why does reversibility happen?

Reversibility occurs when a person is not able to take part in training for a period of time. This could be due to illness, injury or other factors such as going on holiday and not having access to training facilities.

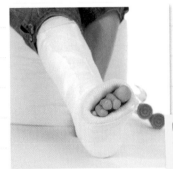

Injury is one of the main reasons that reversibility occurs.

The effects of reversibility on fitness

Reversibility is also known as **detraining**. When a person doesn't take part in training for some time, any training adaptations that have been developed as a result of the training will deteriorate.

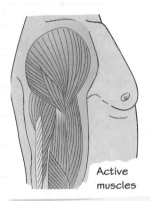 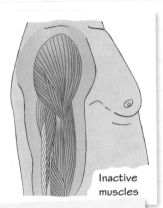

Active muscles   Inactive muscles

The trained muscle on the left is much larger than the untrained muscle on the right.

Overtraining

Overtraining occurs when the training workload is increased too quickly or there are not sufficient periods of rest and recovery.

✓ It leads to a greater risk of injury or of fitness levels not improving due to fatigue, as the body is not able to recover sufficiently between sessions.

✓ It can also mean a person's fitness declines as they are training too much.

Applying the principle of reversibility

A person who has had a period away from training, for whatever reason, will need to work out how this has affected their fitness levels.

- Taking part in fitness tests and comparing their results to previous fitness test results is a good way of doing this.
- They will then need to restart their training programme at a level appropriate to their current, somewhat reduced, fitness levels.

Now try this

Identify **one** reason why an athlete might experience reversibility.

Variation

It is important to add variation to training programmes to avoid boredom and maintain motivation to train.

Varying training routines

Minor changes in routine can produce large fitness gains. This change is known as **variation**.

Some basic things that could be done to ensure variation include changing the:

- type of equipment
- training environment
- order of training
- type of exercise
- nature of your training.

Why is variation important?

Variation is important because it helps to:

☑ keep you interested and maintain the motivation and enjoyment associated with training. If you are doing the same training all the time you are likely to become bored and so more likely to give up

☑ provide new challenges for your body and reduces the risk of injuries caused by the repetition of the same actions and training methods.

Variation in practice

You still need to consider the specificity principle (see page 7) so that any variation is beneficial to the individual and their training goals.

An example of variation in practice is a footballer who uses both bounding ladder drills and weight training to help build both leg power and strength. This will allow for recovery and adaptation to take place while maintaining enjoyment. This way they are more likely to persist with training.

Now try this

Sanjid is a long-distance runner. He runs on his own following the same road-based route to improve his aerobic endurance.

Think about what you could do if you took part in long-distance running to make it a bit more interesting or different and then consider if these may work for Sanjid.

Give **two** examples of how variation could be applied to reduce boredom in Sanjid's training.

Training zones

A training zone is the correct intensity at which a person should exercise in order to experience fitness improvement.

Why are training zones used?

To improve particular components of fitness, the participant must work at a specific training intensity. For example, to train for aerobic fitness, an individual must work at a lower intensity than someone who wants to train for anaerobic fitness.

- Working above or below the specified training zone will result in the incorrect component of fitness being trained.
- If the training zone is at too low a level, there will be no training effect.

Revise the FITT principle of intensity on page 4.

Anaerobic fitness

- Anaerobic fitness is required for sports that don't use oxygen as the main supply of energy, such as the 100 m sprint.
- Anaerobic fitness training is only recommended for people who already have good levels of fitness, as it can be harmful to the health of someone with low levels of fitness.

Percentage of maximum heart rate (Max HR) and training zones

A percentage of Max HR is used to calculate how hard you should work your heart to develop either aerobic or anaerobic fitness.

Warm-up or cool down zone		50–60% of Max HR	This zone can also be used for people new to training and to maintain current fitness levels.
Fat-burning zone		60–70% of Max HR	In this zone, body fat is used to provide energy. It is good for people who wish to lose excess body fat.
Aerobic training zone		70–80% of Max HR	This zone is used to develop aerobic endurance.
Anaerobic training zone		80–100% of Max HR	In this zone, the anaerobic energy systems are used to produce energy.

Calculating heart rates for the training zones

Max HR = 220 – age

50% Max HR = 50/100 × Max HR

60% Max HR = 60/100 × Max HR

70% Max HR = 70/100 × Max HR

80% Max HR = 80/100 × Max HR

100% Max HR = Max HR

Revise methods of measuring and estimating heart rate on page 4.

Now try this

1 Sunita is 22 years old. Calculate her maximum heart rate.
2 Calculate what Sunita's minimum and maximum heart rate should be for training in the aerobic training zone.

Remember to give your answers in beats per minute (bpm) and round your answers to the nearest whole number.

Technology to measure exercise intensity

A range of different types of technology are now available to help people to measure the exercise intensity they are working at. This technology helps to provide reliable, accurate data that can easily be seen while the person is still taking part in exercise.

Heart rate monitor

A heart rate monitor can be used to measure exercise intensity when a person is taking part in exercise.

A strap is worn around the chest that detects the heart rate. The signal is transmitted to a receiver that can be worn on the wrist for an individual to easily see their heart rate when they are taking part in training to measure their exercise intensity.

See page 4 for more on heart rate intensity.

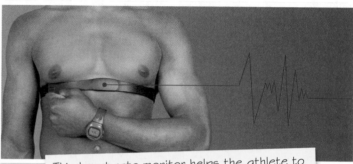

This heart rate monitor helps the athlete to see their exercise intensity at a glance.

Smart watch

A smart watch can be worn around a person's wrist. It provides the user with their current heart rate as well as an overview of the person's heart rate during and post exercise. This can be used to:

- work out if the person was training at the right intensity for the component of fitness they were training
- show how quickly their cardiovascular system recovers from an exercise session.

Wearing a smart watch can help you work out if you are training at the right intensity.

Apps

Many apps are available that can be downloaded and used on smart watches, smartphones or on wearable clothing to help to record exercise intensity.

Many of these apps will allow the individual to select the type of exercise they are taking part in and then set the app to sound an alarm if they are exercising outside of the set training threshold they are targeting to train a specific component of fitness.

Now try this

Explain **one** benefit of using technology to measure exercise intensity.

This question is looking at the advantages of using technology to measure exercise intensity, which usually means recording the heart rate using technology.

Try to give a reason why technology is a benefit.

Fitness testing: importance to sports performers and coaches

It is important for a fitness training programme to focus on the targeted components of fitness. Therefore, fitness testing should be carried out before, during and after the training programme to be able to monitor whether the training is working.

Baseline data

Fitness testing provides **baseline** data from which we can monitor and improve performance.

Baseline data are the scores/results recorded at the start of any training programme.

Over time these tests can be repeated, helping to show improvements and areas for further attention.

Training programme design

Training programmes can be designed to focus on performer's strengths and weaknesses.

For example, if a sprinter has good speed but their reaction time is below average, it gives the coach and athlete an area of training to focus on.

Determine if training programmes are working

Fitness testing also allows you to see if training programmes are working. By repeating the same tests before and after a training block you can see if programmes have been effective.

If fitness test data shows that no improvements are being made to the targeted component of fitness, it confirms that the training programme is not working for the individual.

Baseline data for a gymnast might be used to give the first set of results for flexibility, strength and speed. From this, the coach and performer can then work out which of these components of fitness need to be developed.

Goal-setting aims

Fitness test results can help a performer set themself goals. This can be motivating and will encourage them to work hard in training.

For example, a netball wing attack may set themself a target of improving their Illinois agility run test scores by three seconds over a six-week training period (see page 35). By testing at regular intervals they will be able to see their progress towards the goal to improve their agility.

Provide performers with something to aim for

Taking part in regular training does require a lot of dedication from a performer. So, having key areas to focus on can help to encourage them to put in full effort when they are training and ensure they attend every training session knowing that this training can have a big impact on their fitness test results.

Now try this

Give **one** reason why it is important to record baseline fitness scores.

 Think about what the term baseline means and how this would be relevant for training programmes.

Pre-fitness test procedures: screening

Any fitness programme needs to be safe and appropriate for the person who will be using it. Before carrying out fitness tests, a number of pre-test procedures need to be conducted to ensure you have the essential information about an individual. These include using a PAR-Q and a lifestyle questionnaire.

Physical Activity Readiness Questionnaire (PAR-Q)

A PAR-Q is a questionnaire used to assess a person's medical history. It determines the safety or possible risks based upon the individual answer given.

There are between 8 and 12 questions in a standard PAR-Q, which require a simple 'yes' or 'no' response.

If an individual responds with a 'yes' to any question, they should be encouraged to seek medical clearance from their doctor before beginning an exercise programme.

 Real world

Example of questions from a PAR-Q

- Do you have chest pain when performing physical activity?
- Are you pregnant or have you given birth in the last six months?
- Do you have a bone or joint problem that causes you pain when exercising?
- Have you had recent surgery?
- Are you currently taking prescribed medications for a chronic condition?

Lifestyle questionnaire

This contains questions based on the performer's lifestyle and is used to gain personal information about their lifestyle choices such as:

- current activity levels
- stress levels
- the foods they eat
- drinking alcohol
- smoking.

All of these can impact on their health and the design of the training programme.

Confidentiality

All information that is taken from a sports performer should be kept confidential in line with the latest legal requirements for storing and using other people's personal information.

Pre-fitness checks for participants are revised on page 17.

Informed consent

This is a form that makes the performer aware of what is involved in the exercise testing and any risks there may be. They can then give their agreement or consent to undertake the tests. This then provides documented evidence that shows that participants have been provided with all the necessary information to undertake the test.

The consent form should be signed and dated by the participant and the tester.

An informed consent form confirms that the performer:

👍 is able to follow the test method

👍 knows exactly what is required of them during testing

👍 has fully consented to their participation in the fitness tests

👍 knows that they are able to ask any questions relating to the tests

👍 knows that they are able to withdraw their consent at any time.

Now try this

Why should a PAR-Q be completed before a person takes part in a training programme?

◀ Remember that PAR-Q stands for Physical Activity Readiness Questionnaire.

Pre-fitness test procedures: calibration of equipment and test protocol

Before carrying out fitness tests, you also need to ensure the test protocol is being followed, calibrate equipment and complete a participant pre-fitness check. These ensure that the participant is ready to take part in the tests, and that the test results are valid and reliable (for more on validity and reliability, see page 19).

Test protocol

Each test needs specific equipment. The person carrying out the test needs to follow a **protocol**, which is the set method of administering the test. The protocol includes information related to:

- how the test should be set up
- which equipment needs to be used
- how to complete the test correctly
- how to record the results accurately.

It is important to remember that calibration of equipment is **not** the process of checking if the equipment is broken! It is checking to ensure that it is producing accurate measurements.

Calibration of equipment

This is the process of checking and, if necessary, adjusting pieces of fitness testing equipment to ensure they record data accurately. Equipment should be calibrated regularly to ensure results are valid and accurate.

Scales: use a fixed weight to test they are measuring accurately.

Use a stopwatch to check the beeps from the multi-stage fitness test recording are timed accurately.

Participant pre-fitness check

Before the participant takes part in any fitness tests, the person administering the test should check the following. The participant should:

👍 have medical clearance for any health conditions

👍 be free of injuries

👍 not have taken part in exercise prior to testing other than warm-up exercises

👍 be wearing appropriate clothing

👍 not have had a heavy meal three hours before the test

👍 have had a good night's sleep

👍 not have trained on the day and be fully recovered from previous training

👍 have avoided stimulants such as tea, coffee or nicotine for two hours before the test.

Indoor fitness test location checks

The area where the tests are performed should be:

- at room temperature (around 18 degrees)
- well ventilated
- clean and dust-free.

Now try this

Before taking part in a fitness test, the participant should have completed a PAR-Q questionnaire.

These are checks to ensure the results from the fitness test are not affected by factors related to the participant not being able to perform at their best.

Suggest **three** other participant pre-fitness checks that should be carried out before a participant takes part in a fitness test.

Choosing appropriate fitness tests and interpreting results

Fitness tests should be selected that are appropriate for the individual and the component of fitness being tested. Once the fitness tests have been completed, the results need to be analysed to find out what they show about the participant's component of fitness that is being assessed – this is the process of interpreting fitness test results.

Choosing appropriate fitness tests

When selecting a fitness test for an individual there are a number of factors that should be considered.

Does it measure the targeted component of fitness?

Selecting appropriate fitness tests

Does it replicate movements of the participant's sport?

Is it appropriate for the participant's level of fitness?

 **Example**

Jules is 56 years old and hasn't taken part in sport or exercise for a number of years. She is starting an exercise programme and wants to improve her fitness so she can take part in a 5 km Park Run. Her personal trainer wants to measure her aerobic endurance. He selects the 12-minute Cooper run test for Jules rather than the multi-stage fitness test (MSFT). This is because the Cooper run test allows the participant to run, jog or walk at their own pace, whereas the MSFT provides the pace that they have to travel, which may result in Jules over exerting herself and becoming unwell or becoming demotivated.

To revise the MSFT test, see page 20 and to revise the 12-minute Cooper run test, see page 22.

Recording fitness test results

Once the fitness test has been completed, the results should be recorded accurately (using appropriate templates where needed) and using the correct units of measurement specified in the test protocol.

Interpreting fitness results

Fitness test results are interpreted by comparing an individual's results with other people of the same age group and gender. This is done by using published **normative data tables**.

- This shows whether an individual has lower or higher results than most of the population.
- The normative data tables are produced by calculating the average scores from fitness test results.

Normative data

When measurements of people are taken in a population and plotted on a graph the results form a shape like this. Most people's results are in the middle.

Normative data curve

Age	Excellent	Above average
13–14	>2700 m	2400–2700 m
15–16	>2900 m	2500–2800 m
17–19	>3000 m	2700–3000 m
20–29	>2800 m	2400–2800 m
30–39	>2700 m	2300–2700 m
40–49	>2500 m	2100–2500 m
>50	>2400 m	2000–2400 m

Part of a table showing normative data for male athletes

Now try this

Why is it important to select fitness tests that are appropriate for the participant's level of fitness?

 These factors are there to make sure the test being selected will get the best results for that participant's needs.

Reliability, validity and practicality of fitness testing

Part of the process of fitness testing requires the person administering the test to ensure the fitness test results are reliable and valid. The practicality of the fitness testing should also be considered.

Validity

Validity is how accurate a set of results are. That is, do the results really measure what we want them to?

This can also be applied to the part of the body being tested or how closely the fitness test replicates the participant's sport.

 Example

A javelin thrower has to have high levels of flexibility in their shoulders to be able to throw the javelin long distances. The sit and reach test (see page 26) measures flexibility of the lower back and hamstrings. If a javelin thrower took part in a sit and reach fitness test it would not provide a valid assessment of the flexibility of their shoulders.

Reliability

Reliability is the ability to repeatedly carry out the same test and expect comparable results each time.

Things that can influence reliability when a participant is taking part in follow-up fitness tests are:

- calibration of equipment
- motivation of the participant
- conditions of the testing environment (indoor versus outdoor conditions; weather conditions)
- experience of the person administering the test
- whether the standardised test procedures are followed
- length and type of warm-up
- time of day
- amount of sleep the subject has had
- different clothing or footwear worn by the participant.

 **Example**

If a participant took part in a multi-stage fitness test outside and then repeated the test in an indoor location, the results of the test could be different due to the change in fitness test location conditions.

Fitness testing outside could be affected by factors such as the weather and the running surface being wet or slippery, so could have a negative effect on performance.

Practicality

Practicality refers to how suitable the test is for the given situation, the person administering the test and the people taking part in the test.

Things to consider when taking into account practicality include:

- cost
- time taken to perform the test
- time taken to set up the test
- time taken to analyse data
- number of participants that can take part in the test at the same time.

 Example

A football coach may find fitness tests that can be carried out by the whole team at the same time have more practicality for them, as they will take less time to administer compared with fitness tests that have to be carried out one person at a time.

Now try this

You are working as a fitness coach for a football team. Having completed the multi-stage fitness test six weeks ago in a sports hall, you want to test the football team again to check for improvements.

List **three** things you should consider to ensure the test is reliable.

Remember, reliability is ensuring the test conditions and participant pre-fitness test check are as similar as possible to previous testing processes.

19

Fitness tests for aerobic endurance: multi-stage fitness test and Yo-Yo test

The multi-stage fitness test (MSFT) is a **maximal test**, which means the participant continues until they are exhausted. It is also known as the bleep test and it assesses aerobic endurance by predicting maximum oxygen uptake.

Characteristics

- Measures: your predicted maximum oxygen uptake (aerobic endurance).
- Unit: level reached.
- Equipment: non-slip surface, tape measure, cones, the MSFT CD or app, pen, paper to record results.
- Used by: long-distance runners, long-distance cyclists.

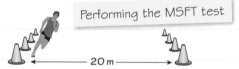

Performing the MSFT test

← 20 m →

Three versions

- Version 1 is for beginners with slower beeps.
- Version 2 is for participants with higher levels of aerobic endurance with faster beeps.
- Version 3 is called the **intermittent Yo-Yo test**. It includes brief active recovery periods, which replicates performance in game-based intermittent sports such as netball.

Oxygen intake

VO$_2$ max is the maximum amount of oxygen a person's body is able to take in and use. It is measured in ml/kg/min and is the best measure of aerobic fitness.

MSFT protocol

1 Allow performers to complete a warm-up.

2 Using the tape to measure, place two cones 20 m apart on a flat surface.

3 Stand on the start line. After the triple beep, run slowly to the other cone before the next beep.

4 After the beep, run back to the other cone. Do not get ahead of the beeps.

5 Run faster as the beeps get closer together.

6 Keep running until you are physically exhausted or have failed to reach the cone by the time the beep has sounded three times.

7 Record the level (L) and shuttle (S) reached.

Use this information to predict your VO$_2$ max.

Interpreting results

	Age	Excellent	Above average	Average	Below average	Poor
Male	17–20	L12; S12	L11; S6	L9; S2	L7; S6	<L7; S3
	21–30	L12; S12	L11; S7	L9; S3	L7; S8	<L7; S5
	31–40	L11; S7	L10; S4	L6; S10	L6; S7	<L6; S4
	41–50	L10; S4	L9; S4	L6; S9	L5; S9	<L5; S2
Female	17–20	L10; S11	L9; S3	L6; S8	L5; S2	<L4; S9
	21–30	L10; S8	L9; S2	L6; S6	L5; S1	<L4; S9
	31–40	L10; S4	L8; S7	L6; S3	L4; S6	<L4; S5
	41–50	L9; S9	L7; S2	L5; S7	L4; S2	<L4; S1

For the intermittent Yo-Yo test there is an active recovery period after each 2 × 20 m run.

Normative data results for the MSFT test for adults aged 17–50.

Reliability, validity and practicality

Reliability	Validity
• Motivation will affect reliability, as this is a maximal test. • Distance must be measured accurately each time. • Conditions of the test environment must be same each time.	👍 High level for sports that involve running 👎 Low level for non-running sports, e.g. swimming.
	Practicality
	👍 low cost 👍 easy to set up. 👍 large numbers can take part

Now try this

Explain why measuring too short a distance for the MSFT would affect the reliability of the test results.

Fitness tests for aerobic endurance: Harvard step test

The Harvard step test measures the person's ability to recover from strenuous exercise. It is a **submaximal** test, which means the participant does not have to exercise to exhaustion.

Characteristics

- Measures: your predicted maximum oxygen uptake (aerobic endurance).
- Unit: total number of heart beats in a 30-second period.
- Used by: 5000 m runners, long-distance cyclists.
- Equipment: a 45 cm high bench, stopwatch, metronome, heart rate monitor if available. Pen, paper to record the results.

45 cm

Performing the Harvard step test

Test protocol

1 Allow performers to complete a warm-up.

2 Start the metronome to provide a stepping pace for stepping onto the bench every two seconds.

3 Give the command 'go' and start the stopwatch.

4 The participant steps up onto the bench and down in time to the metronome.

5 The test is stopped after 5 minutes, or sooner if the participant is not able to continue for the full test duration.

6 One minute after the test has stopped, record the participant's heart rate – pulse 1.

7 Two minutes after the test has stopped, record the participant's heart rate – pulse 2.

8 Three minutes after the test has stopped, record the participant's heart rate – pulse 3.

9 Use the equation to work out the result:
$$\frac{30000}{(\text{pulse 1} + \text{pulse 2} + \text{pulse 3})} = \text{Result}$$

Interpreting results

	Excellent	Above average	Average	Below average	Poor
Male	>90.0	80.0–90.0	65.0–79.9	55.0–64.9	<55
Female	>86.0	76.0–86.0	61.0–75.9	50.0–60.9	<50

Normative data results for the Harvard step test for 16-year-olds

Reliability, validity and practicality

Reliability	Validity
• Motivation will affect reliability. • Environmental conditions do not affect reliability: the test is carried out indoors. • Conditions must be the same each time. • Standardised procedures: equipment, warm-up, stepping pace must be the same each time. • The participant's pulse must be measured at the correct time.	👎 Shorter or heavier participants may need to work harder, as the height of the bench is always the same. 👎 Minimal replication of sports movements. **Practicality** 👍 Low cost 👍 Easy to set up 👍 Large numbers can take part.

Now try this

A person takes part in the Harvard step test. Their results are: Pulse 1 = 140 bpm Pulse 2 = 128 bpm Pulse 3 = 110 bpm

Identify the Harvard step test result for this participant.

Had a look ☐ Nearly there ☐ Nailed it! ☐

Fitness tests for aerobic endurance: 12-minute Cooper test

The Cooper run/swim test involves running or swimming for 12 minutes and the distance covered is recorded. It is a submaximal test, which means the participant does not have to exercise to exhaustion.

Characteristics

- Measures: predicted maximum oxygen uptake (aerobic endurance).
- Units: metres.
- Equipment: stop watch, athletics track for the run or swimming pool for the swim, cones (for the run), whistle, stop watch, tape measure, pen and paper to record and an assistant to administer.
- Used by: runners, swimmers, footballers.

Interpreting results

Cooper test results for males (in meters)					
Age	Excellent	Above Ave	Average	Below Ave	Poor
Male 20-29	>2800 m	2400–2800 m	2200–2399 m	1600–2199 m	<1600 m
Males 30-39	>2700 m	2300–2700 m	1900–2299 m	1500–1999 m	<1500 m
Males 40-49	>2500 m	2100–2500 m	1700–2099 m	1400–1699 m	<1400 m
Males 50+	>2400 m	2000–2400 m	1600–1999 m	1300–1599 m	<1300 m
Cooper test results for females (in meters)					
Age	Excellent	Above Ave	Average	Below Ave	Poor
Females 20-29	>2700 m	2200–2700 m	1800–2199 m	1500–1799 m	<1500 m
Females 30-39	>2500 m	2000–2500 m	1700–1999 m	1400–1699 m	<1400 m
Females 40-49	>2300 m	1900–2300 m	1500–1899 m	1200–1499 m	<1200 m
Females 50+	>2200 m	1700–2200 m	1400–1699 m	1100–1399 m	<1100 m

Normative data table for 12-minute Cooper run test

12-minute run test protocol

1. The participant stands at the starting line on the athletics track.
2. Blow a whistle for the participant to start running around the track.
3. At 12 minutes, blow the whistle again for the participant to stop running.
4. Place a cone at the point where the participant stopped running.
5. Measure the distance covered and record it to the nearest 10 m.

12-minute swim test protocol

1. The participant stands at the edge of the swimming pool.
2. Blow a whistle for the participant to dive into the pool and start swimming.
3. At 12 minutes, blow the whistle again for the participant to stop swimming.
4. Place a cone at the point where the participant stopped swimming.
5. Measure the distance covered and record it to the nearest 10 m.

Reliability, validity and practicality

Reliability	Validity
• Motivation will affect reliability. • Environmental conditions could affect reliability if the Cooper run test is conducted outdoors. • Conditions of test environment must be same each time. • The administrator does not need experience as the test is simple to administer.	👍 High levels for sports that involve running or swimming 👍 Replicates the movement in running and swimming.
	Practicality
	Low cost 👍 Easy to set up. 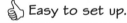 Large numbers can take part.

Now try this

Explain why the 12-minute Cooper run test may be more appropriate for a person with low levels of fitness rather than the multi-stage fitness test.

Fitness tests for muscular endurance: one-minute press-up test

Fitness tests can be used to assess muscular endurance. The press-up test is used to measure localised muscular endurance in the upper body.

Characteristics

- Measures: endurance of the upper body.
- Units: reps per minute.
- Equipment: exercise mat and a stopwatch, pen and paper, assistant to administer the test.
- Used for: boxing, rowing, climbing, basketball, netball.

Full press-up

Performing the one-minute press-up test

Modified press-up

A slightly less-challenging version of the test can be done in a bent knee position

Test protocol

1 Ask the participant to take up a full press-up position. Their arms should be fully extended.

2 Set the timer for one minute. Ask the participant to complete as many full press-ups as they can in this time.

3 A full press-up is one where the elbows are bent to 90° and then fully extended.

Interpreting results: Full press-up

Rating	Men (reps/minute)	Women (reps/minute)
Excellent	>45	>34
Good	35–44	17–33
Average	20–34	6–16
Poor	<19	<5

Normative data results for the full press-up test

Modified press-up

Rating	Number of reps
Excellent	>39
Good	34–38
Average	17–33
Fair	6–16
Poor	<6

Normative data results for the modified press-up test

Reliability, validity and practicality

Reliability	Validity
• Motivation will affect reliability. • Environmental conditions do not affect reliability: carried out indoors. • Standardised test procedures: correct position; equipment, warm-up, must be the same for each test. • Conditions of test environment must be the same each time (e.g. surface). • Administrator does not need experience.	👍 High levels for sports that require muscular endurance in the upper body, such as rowing, netball and basketball 👍 Ensure the type of press-up has been noted.
	Practicality
	👍 Low cost 👍 Easy to set up 👍 Large numbers can take part.

Now try this

Anita takes part in the one-minute press-up test on two different occasions. On the first occasion she performs the test using the modified press-up technique. On the second occasion she uses the full press-up technique.

Look at the normative data results table to help you work this out.

1 Why would using different press-up techniques affect the reliability of the fitness test results?

2 Anita's result for the one-minute full press-up test was 15 reps per minute. What is her rating according to the normative data table?

Fitness tests for muscular endurance: one-minute sit-up test

Fitness tests can be used to assess muscular endurance. The one-minute sit-up test is used to measure localised muscular endurance in the abdominals.

Characteristics

- Measures: endurance of the abdominal muscles.
- Units: reps per minute.
- Equipment: exercise mat and a stopwatch, pen and paper, test administrator.
- Used by: boxers, kayakers, gymnasts.

Performing the one-minute sit-up test

Test protocol

1 Perform a warm-up.

2 Lie on the mat with your knees bent and your feet flat on the floor. Your feet can be held by a partner if required.

3 Fold your arms across your body.

4 Use an assistant to time you for one minute.

5 Complete as many full sit-ups as you can in this time.

6 A full sit-up is one where you raise yourself up to 90° and then lower yourself back to the floor.

Interpreting results

Rating	Males	Females
Excellent	49–59	42–54
Good	43–48	36–41
Above average	39–42	32–35
Average	35–38	28–31
Below average	31–34	24–27
Poor	25–30	18–23
Very poor	11–24	3–17

Normative data results for the one-minute sit-up test

Reliability, validity and practicality

Reliability	Validity
• Motivation will affect reliability • Environmental conditions do not affect reliability: carried out indoors • Standardised test procedures: equipment, warm-up, position must be the same for each test • Conditions of test environment must be the same each time (e.g. surface) • Administrator does not need experience.	👍 High levels for most sports as it tests the endurance of core muscle, which are needed for performance in many sports.
	Practicality
	👍 Low cost 👍 Easy to set up 👍 Large numbers can take part 👎 Not suitable for participants with back injuries.

Now try this

Mina completes the sit-up test. The first time her friend holds her feet, the second time she completes the test on her own.

1 Identify **one** impact of this change in fitness test method.

2 Mina's results for the sit-up test are 39. What is her rating?

Have a go at completing a sit-up with a partner holding your feet and then again without a partner and compare the two methods – is it more difficult to perform the sit-up with or without a partner?

Fitness tests for muscular endurance: timed plank test

Fitness tests can be used to assess muscular endurance. The timed plank test is used to measure localised muscular endurance in the abdominals. This is a maximal test so the person completes the test until they are exhausted.

Characteristics

- Measures: endurance of the abdominal muscles.
- Units: seconds.
- Equipment: exercise mat and a stopwatch, pen and paper and person to administer the test.
- Used by: rugby players, martial arts, gymnasts.

Performing the timed plank test. The person holds the plank position for as long as possible.

Test protocol

1 Perform a warm-up.

2 Start with the upper body supported on the mat by the elbows and forearms. Legs and back should be straight, hips lifted off the floor and head looking forwards, toes holding the lower body weight.

3 As soon as the position is assumed, the assistant starts the stopwatch.

4 Remain in this position for as long as possible.

5 The test is stopped when the person is not able to maintain the position.

6 The time the plank position was maintained for is the score for the test.

Interpreting results

Rating	Time
Excellent	>6 minutes
Very good	4–6 minutes
Above average	2–4 minutes
Average	1–2 minutes
Below average	30–60 seconds
Poor	12–30 seconds
Very poor	< 15 seconds

Normative data results for the timed plank test for males and females

Reliability, validity and practicality

Reliability	Validity
• Motivation will affect reliability • Environmental conditions do not affect reliability: carried out indoors • Conditions of test environment must be the same each time (e.g. surface) • Correct position must be maintained • Administrator does not need experience.	👍 High levels for most sports as it tests the endurance of core muscle, which are needed for performance in many sports 👍 It is a maximal test so will test sports performers with high levels of fitness.

	Practicality
	👍 Low cost 👍 Easy to set up 👍 Large numbers can take part.

Now try this

Izzy takes part in horse riding.
She performs the timed plank test and gets a score of 45 seconds.

Identify the rating for this score.

Use the normative data table to work out what rating the 45-second time period fits into.

Fitness tests for flexibility: sit and reach test

The sit and reach test measures flexibility in a localised area: the lower back and hamstrings

Characteristics

- Measures: flexibility in the lower back and hamstrings.
- Units: cm or inches.
- Equipment: sit and reach box, exercise mat, pen, paper and test administrator.
- Used by: gymnasts, hurdlers, martial artists.

Performing the sit and reach test

> Many fitness tests are specific. Make sure you know what they are measuring. For example, the sit and reach test would not help you measure shoulder flexibility.

Test protocol

1 Complete a warm-up (muscles will be more pliable and flexible if fully warmed up).

2 Use a sit and reach box.

3 Remove shoes and sit with straight legs and feet flat against the sit and reach box.

4 In a slow, steady movement, stretch forward and reach as far as possible with your hands, sliding them on top of the box and pushing the slider forwards.

5 Hold the slider and keep your knees straight throughout.

6 Record distance reached.

Interpreting results

Gender	Excellent	Above average	Average	Below average	Poor
Male	>14	14.0–11.0	10.9–7.0	6.9–4.0	<4
Female	>15	15.0–12.0	11.9–7.0	6.9–4.0	<4

> Normative data results for the sit and reach test results (in cm) for 16–19-year-olds

Reliability, validity and practicality

Reliability	Validity
• Motivation will affect reliability • Environmental conditions do not affect reliability: carried out indoors • Conditions of test environment must be the same each time (e.g. surface) • Standardised test procedures: warm-up must be the same for each test; maintain correct position • Administrator does not need experience.	👍 High for sports that need lower body flexibility 👎 Low for sports that need upper body flexibility, e.g. swimming 👎 Variations in trunk and arm length can make comparisons hard.

Practicality
👍 Low cost   👍 Easy to set up. 👎 Only one person can take the test if there is only one box available

Now try this

1 Why do you think a hurdler's score in the sit and reach test would be high?

2 Kyoko completes the sit and reach test. Her result is 13.5 cm. What is her rating?

> Think about the action a hurdler has to use when they are jumping over hurdles and how this could affect the flexibility of their hamstrings and lower back.

Fitness tests for flexibility: calf muscle flexibility test

The calf flexibility test measures flexibility in a localised area: the lower part of the leg – the gastrocnemius and soleus muscles in the calf.

Characteristics

- Measures: flexibility in the lower part of the leg.
- Equipment: wall, tape measure, pen, paper and person to administer the test.
- Units: cm/mm.
- Used by: footballers, basketballers.

Performing the calf muscle flexibility test

Test protocol

1 Complete a warm-up, including stretching (the warmer the muscles are the more pliable, and therefore more flexible, they will be).

2 The participant stands a short distance from the wall.

3 They stand with one foot in front of the other, both feet pointing forwards and both heels on the ground.

4 Keeping the heel of the front foot on the ground, the person should bend their knee so that it touches the wall.

5 The person moves a little further away from the wall and repeats the process, attempting to touch their knee to the wall.

6 This is repeated until the person is no longer able to touch their knee to the wall.

7 The distance from the front of the toe to the wall is recorded at the maximum distance the knee could touch the wall.

8 Repeat the test on the other leg.

Interpreting results

There are no normative data tables for this test; however, the test can be used by individuals to compare their own test results to check if a flexibility training programme they are carrying out is helping to increase the flexibility in their calves.

Reliability, validity and practicality

Reliability	Validity
• Motivation is not a key factor	👍 High for sports that require flexibility in the lower body
• Environmental conditions do not affect reliability: carried out indoors	👍 High for health-related fitness, e.g. football, track events
• Conditions of test environment must be the same each time (e.g. surface)	👎 Low validity where high levels of flexibility are required in the upper body.
• The warm-up must be the same for each test	**Practicality**
• The correct position must be maintained	👍 Low cost
• Administrator does not need experience.	👍 Easy to set up
	👍 Large numbers can take part.

Now try this

Identify what sport may require high levels of flexibility in the muscles at the back of the lower leg.

The muscles at the back of the lower leg are the gastrocnemius and soleus.

Fitness tests for flexibility: shoulder flexibility test

The shoulder flexibility test measures flexibility in a localised area: the shoulder in the upper body.

Characteristics

- Measures: range of movement in the shoulder joints.
- Equipment: rope, tape measure, pen, paper and person to administer test.
- Units: inches.
- Used by: swimmers, gymnasts.

Performing the shoulder flexibility test

Test protocol

1 Complete a warm-up (the warmer the muscles are the more pliable, and therefore more flexible, they will be).

2 Hold the rope with both hands 4 inches apart.

3 Hold both arms out in front of the body in line with the chest.

4 Rotate the arms so that they travel up and over the head and down towards the back.

5 As the arms travel backwards and resistance is felt, slide the hands further away from each other to allow the movement to continue.

6 Stop the movement when the rope touches the back.

7 Return arms to their starting position while not allowing the hands to move along the rope.

8 Measure the distance along the rope between the two thumbs to the nearest ¼ inch.

9 Measure the width of the person's shoulders at the furthest point of each deltoid to the nearest ¼ inch.

10 Subtract the shoulder measurement from the rope measurement.

11 Repeat the test three times and record the greatest distance achieved in the test.

Interpreting results

Rating	Men	Women
Excellent	<7.00	<5.00
Good	11.50–7.00	9.75–5.00
Average	14.50–11.49	13.00–9.74
Fair	19.75–14.49	17.75–12.99
Poor	>19.75	>17.75

Shoulder flexibility test results (in inches) for adults

Reliability, validity and practicality

Reliability	Validity
• Motivation is not a key factor • Environmental conditions do not affect reliability: carried out indoors • Correct position must be maintained • Warm-up must be the same for each test • Administrator does not need experience	👍 High for sports that need shoulder joint flexibility, e.g. swimming, javelin or tennis 👍 Low where lower body flexibility is required.
	Practicality
	👍 Low cost 👍 Easy to set up. 👍 Large numbers can take part

Now try this

Nikki tests her shoulder flexibility. Her result is 5.25. What is her test result rating?

Fitness tests for speed: 30 m sprint tests

The 30m sprint tests measure speed from a standing start or a running start (flying sprint).

Characteristics

- Measures: sprint speed.
- Units: seconds (s).
- Equipment: two cones, tape measure, stopwatch, flat non-slip surface.
- Used by: any sports that require speed, such as sprinting, netball, rugby football.

30 m sprint test protocol

1. Complete a warm-up.

2. Measure out a 30 m straight line.

3. Mark both ends with cones.

4. Place your foot on or behind the starting line, and take up the sprint position.

5. On the timer's command, sprint to the other cone.

6. The time is recorded from the moment you start to the moment you cross the finish line.

7. Conduct the test three times with a three-minute recovery between each test.

8. Take the fastest time as the score.

30 m flying sprint test protocol

1. Complete a warm-up.

2. Measure 30 m and 60 m in straight lines.

3. Mark each measurement with a cone.

4. Take up the sprint start position at one end.

5. On the timer's command, run to the first cone.

6. Start the stopwatch and time how long it takes for the person to complete the first 30 m and also the full 60 m distance.

7. Conduct the test three times with a three-minute recovery between each test.

8. Take the fastest time as the score.

Interpreting results

Gender	Excellent	Above Average	Average	Below Average	Poor
Male	<2.6 secs	2.6–2.9 secs	2.9–3.1 secs	3.1–3.3 secs	>3.3 secs
Female	<3.0 secs	3.0–3.3 secs	3.3–3.5 secs	3.5–3.7 secs	>3.7 secs

30 m sprint results (in seconds) for adults.

Rating	Men	Women
Excellent	<4.0	<4.5
Good	4.2–4.0	4.6–4.5
Average	4.4–4.3	4.8–4.7
Fair	4.6–4.5	5.0–4.9
Poor	>4.6	>5.0

30 m flying sprint results (in seconds)

Reliability, validity and practicality

Reliability	Validity
• Motivation will affect reliability • Environmental conditions do not affect reliability: carried out indoors • Conditions must be the same each time (e.g. surface, measuring method) • Reliability improved if timing gates are used rather than a stopwatch • Administrator does not need experience.	👍 More valid for a 100 m sprinter than a cyclist as it is a better replication of their sport 👎 It may not be long enough for participants to reach full speed.

	Practicality
	👍 Minimal equipment 👍 Easy to set up 👎 Only one person can take the test at a time.

Now try this

Fatima wants to use the 30 m sprint test to measure improvements in speed as a result of training. The first test was conducted in a sports hall and the second on a field.

What would make the two experiences different?

Give **two** examples of how reliability may have been compromised.

Fitness tests for strength: grip dynamometer test

Fitness tests can also be used to measure strength. The grip dynamometer test measures the strength of the grip-squeezing muscles of the hand.

Characteristics

- Measures: strength of the grip-squeezing muscles of the hand.
- Units: KgW (kilogram weight).
- Equipment: a spring device – a grip dynamometer.
- Used by: sports that require grip strength such as tennis, cricket, squash, baseball.

> You must remember to use the same hand each time so that the result is reliable.

Test protocol

1 Use your dominant hand.

2 Adjust the hand grip size so the dynamometer is comfortable.

3 Stand up with your arms by your body.

4 Hold the dynamometer parallel to the side of your body, with the display facing away from you.

5 Squeeze as hard as possible for five seconds, without moving your arm. (When you apply force, the spring in the dynamometer is compressed and the needle moves, indicating the result.)

6 Carry out three trials, with a one-minute rest between trials.

Interpreting results

Rating	Males aged 15–19 years (KgW)	Females aged 15–19 years (KgW)
Excellent	>52	>32
Good	47–51	28–31
Average	44–46	25–27
Below average	39–43	20–24
Poor	<39	<20

> Hand grip results in KgW for 15–19-year-olds

Reliability, validity and practicality

Reliability	Validity
• Motivation will affect reliability • Environmental conditions do not affect reliability: carried out indoors • Conditions of test environment must be the same each time (e.g. maintain correct position; use same hand; same amount of rest time).	👍 High levels for racquet sports 👎 Low validity for sports that don't require hand grip, e.g. sprinting. **Practicality** 👍 Easy to set up 👎 Only one person can take the test at a time 👎 Requires specialist equipment.

Now try this

Antoni gets a score of 42 KgW in the grip dynamometer test.

Using the table above, what does this tell you about his grip strength?

> Make sure you refer to the correct sex of the person when using the normative data tables to obtain a rating for a result.

Fitness tests for strength: one rep max test

A performer's strength from any muscle group can be measured using the one rep max (1RM) fitness test.

Characteristics

- Measures: strength. Can measure strength in targeted muscle or muscle group. It is a maximal test.
- Units: kg.
- Equipment: fixed or free weights, pen and paper to record and a person to spot.
- Used by: weight-lifting, gymnastics, rugby.

The one rep max test is the amount of weight that can be lifted in a single repetition.

1RM tests for different muscle groups

Type of lift	Muscle(s) targeted
Bench press	Pectorals and triceps
Bicep curl	Biceps
Hamstring curl	Hamstring
Quadricep extension	Quadriceps
Lat pull-down	Latissimus dorsi
Shoulder press	Deltoids

Test protocol

1 Complete a warm-up and an informed consent form.

2 Select a weight lift exercise that targets the muscle or muscle group that is to be tested.

3 The participant should select a weight they can lift and complete that exercise once (one rep).

4 After a two-minute rest period the test is repeated with a heavier weight.

5 The spotter stands in close proximity to the participant so they are ready to support the weight if the participant is not able to complete the lift.

6 Continue until a maximum weight is successfully lifted.

7 This weight is recorded as the one rep max (1RM).

Interpreting results

There are various normative data tables for this test, which can be used to compare test results to check whether a muscular strength training programme is helping to increase strength in the targeted muscle group.

Rating	Males	Females
Excellent	>1.26	>0.78
Good	1.17–1.25	0.72–0.77
Average	0.97–1.16	0.59–0.71
Fair	0.88–0.96	0.53–0.58
Poor	<0.87	<0.52

Normative data results for the 1RM bench press

Reliability, validity and practicality

Reliability	Validity
• Motivation will affect reliability • Environmental conditions do not affect reliability: carried out indoors • Conditions of test environment must be the same each time (e.g. position; rest period) • The administrator must know how to spot weight-lifting to ensure safety • Participant must be familiar with the specific techniques to ensure correct technique.	👍 High levels for a variety of sports as it can be used to test strength in muscles used in the participant's sport.
	Practicality
	👎 Requires access to specialist equipment 👎 Requires an experienced administrator 👎 Only one person can take the test at a time.

Now try this

Tajo performs the bench press test. His 1RM result is 1.20 kg.

What is his 1RM rating?

Check the normative data table above to help you interpret the result.

Fitness tests for body composition: body mass index (BMI)

Body mass index (BMI) is one of the tests used to measure body composition.

Characteristics

- Measures: whether weight is appropriate to height.
- Units: kg/m^2.
- Equipment: measuring scales and a tape measure.
- Used by: netball players, 1500 m runners.

BMI testing is not the best way of testing the body composition of a muscular individual, such as the boxer in this image.

Test protocol

1 Measure your body weight in kilograms.

2 Measure your height in metres.

3 Use the formula: $\dfrac{\text{body weight (kg)}}{\text{height (m)}} \times \text{height (m)}$.

BMI categories

Category	BMI kg/m²
Underweight	<18.5
Healthy weight	18.5–24.9
Overweight	>40

 Real world **Interpreting the results**

If Ben is 1.6 m tall and weighs 62 kg his BMI would be:

$$\frac{62}{1.6} \times 1.6 = 24 \, kg/m^2$$

Looking at the table above, this means that he is a healthy weight for his height.

Make sure you can remember and use the calculation to work out BMI.

Reliability, validity and practicality

Reliability	Validity
• Motivation will not affect reliability • Environmental conditions do not affect reliability: carried out indoors • Does not require the administrator to have experience • Standardised test procedures: scales properly calibrated, height and weight correctly measured.	👎 Not always an accurate measure of body composition as it does not take muscle mass into account. Muscle is heavier than fat so a muscular athlete with very little body fat could be considered obese.
	Practicality
	👍 Low cost 👍 Quick and easy to perform 👍 Does not require participant to remove clothing.

 Now try this

Sarah takes part in sprinting. Her coach carries out a BMI test and the test results show she is very overweight.

Explain if this BMI test is a valid test for body composition for a sprinter.

Remember, a sprinter will have a high muscle mass as their sport requires high levels of strength.

Fitness tests for body composition: bioelectrical impedance analysis

Bioelectrical impedance analysis (BIA) is one test used to measure body composition.

Characteristics

Bioelectrical impedance analysis measures the resistance encountered by a small electrical current passed through your body.

- Measures: percentage body fat.
- Units: % body fat.
- Equipment: BIA machine, pen, paper, someone to administer.
- Used by: boxers, divers, sprinters.

How it works

Fat-free mass lets the current pass through the body more easily compared to fat tissue, therefore the higher the resistance recorded by the BIA machine, the higher the body fat the person has.

Hand-to-foot BIA machine. The electrode is placed on the hand and foot, and the hand moved away from the body.

Test protocol

1. There are different types of bioelectrical impedance analysis machines available so the protocol will be determined by the type of machine used.

2. The machines contain electrodes that come into contact with the skin of the user to send a small electrical current around their body.

3. Ensure the participant is properly hydrated as dehydration can result in a higher body fat reading.

Interpreting results

Description	Women	Men
Essential fat	10–13%	2–5%
Athletes	14–20%	6–13%
Fitness	21–24%	14–17%
Acceptable	25–31%	18–24%
Obesity	>32%	>25%

Normative data results for percentage of body fat for adult women and men

Types of machine

- Hand-held machines – allow the user to hold the machine in front of them.
- Foot-to-foot machines – often integrated into weighing scales to provide the user with their body weight and body fat percentage.
- Hand-to-foot machines – the user holds on to hand grips and footplates.

Reliability, validity and practicality

Reliability	Validity
• Motivation will not affect reliability • Environmental conditions do not affect reliability: carried out indoors • Does not require the administrator to have experience of the testing equipment. • The participant should be properly hydrated • The participant should not have taken part in vigorous exercise in the 12 hours prior to testing.	👍 High level for testing body composition as it measures body fat 👍 Hand-to-foot machines may have higher validity than other types of machines as these may better reflect the whole body composition.
	Practicality
	👍 Quick to perform　👍 Easy to set up 👎 Only one person can take the test at a time　👎 Requires specialist equipment.

Now try this

What factors may reduce the reliability of bioelectrical impedance analysis?

Fitness tests for body composition: waist-to-hip ratio

Waist-to-hip ratio (WHR) uses body measurements to measure body composition.

Characteristics

- Measures: the circumference of the waist and the hips to determine percentage body fat.
- Units: cm (waist-to-hip ratio).
- Equipment: tape measure, pen and paper.

How it works

This test was devised as a way to assess if a person is at risk of coronary heart disease. This assumes that a person at risk of coronary heart disease will have high levels of body fat stored around their waist, which indicates high levels of fat are also stored around the heart.

Test protocol

1 Stand up straight and breathe out, then measure the circumference of the waist just above the belly button with a tape measure. This should be where the waist is smallest – record the measurement.

2 Stand up straight and wrap a tape measure around the widest part of the hips. Do not pull it too tight and record the measurement.

3 Calculate the waist-to-hip ratio by dividing the waist circumference by the hip circumference.

$$\text{Ratio} = \frac{\text{Waist}}{\text{Hips}}$$

Measuring the waist-to-hip ratio

🌐 Real world **Example**

If waist circumference is 80 cm and hip circumference is 90 cm, the WHR ratio is:

80 ÷ 90 = 0.89 cm

Interpreting results

Hip ratio Male	Hip ratio Female	Related health risks
0.95 or below	0.80 or below	Low risk
0.96 to 1.0	0.81 to 0.85	Moderate risk
1.0+	0.85+	High risk

Normative data for the waist-to-hip ratio

Reliability, validity and practicality

Reliability	Validity
• Motivation will not affect reliability • Environmental conditions do not affect reliability: carried out indoors • Conditions of test environment must be the same each time (e.g. measuring method) • Standardised test procedures: must measure the circumference of the body area and not pull the tape too tightly • Administrator does not need experience.	👍 Good for indicating body health 👍 Good for tracking improvements to body composition, as measurements provide a whole body overview 👎 Less useful for targeted sports performance.

	Practicality
	👍 No specialist equipment needed 👍 Easy to set up 👍 No assistant needed.

Now try this

Tyrone completes a waist-to-hip ratio fitness test. His results are: Waist 32 cm   Hips 34 cm

State his waist-to-hip ratio.

Remember to show your working out for any calculations.

Fitness tests for agility: Illinois agility run test

Fitness tests can also be used to measure components of skill-related fitness. The Illinois agility run test measures **agility**, which is the ability of a person to change direction at pace and still maintain their balance.

Characteristics

- Measures: agility.
- Units: seconds(s).
- Used by: rugby, basketball and netball players.
- Equipment: tape measure, stopwatch and eight cones, pen and paper and person to administer the test.

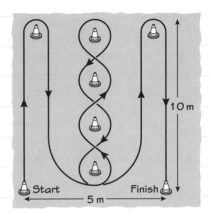

There is a specific layout for the Illinois agility test.

Test protocol

1. Carry out a suitable warm-up.

2. Measure the course as 10 m long by 5 m wide, with cones laid out as shown above.

3. Lie face down by the start cone.

4. On 'go', get up and run around the course, following the line, as quickly as possible.

5. The stopwatch is stopped and your time recorded when you pass the finish cone.

Interpreting results

Gender	Excellent	Above average	Average	Below average	Poor
Male	<15.2	15.2–16.1	16.2–18.1	18.2–19.3	>19.3
Female	<17.0	17.0–17.9	18.0–21.7	21.8–23.0	>23.0

Normative data for the Illinois agility run test results for 16–19-year-olds (in seconds)

Reliability, validity and practicality

Reliability	Validity
• Motivation will affect reliability • Environmental conditions do not affect reliability: carried out indoors • Conditions of test environment must be the same each time (e.g. warm-up; non-slip surface; distance between cones) • Administrator does not need experience.	👍 High levels for sports that require dodging movements, e.g. rugby or netball.

Practicality
👍 Minimal equipment
👍 Easy to set up
👎 Requires a person to help with timing
👎 Only one person can take the test at a time.

Now try this

Selma carries out the Illinois agility test. Her speed is 17.5.

Use the normative data table to work out her result.

Fitness tests for agility: T test

The T test is an alternative test for agility that involves running in different directions.

Characteristics

- Measures: agility.
- Units: seconds (s).
- Equipment: tape measure, stopwatch and four cones, pen and paper and person to administer the test.
- Used by: sports that involve running in different directions, e.g. hockey, tennis, badminton.

How it works

The T test involves running forwards, backwards and sideways in the fastest time possible, compared to the Illinois agility run test, which only includes running forwards and in a circular motion.

Test protocol

1 The participant starts at the cone marked A.

2 The participant should always be facing forwards throughout the test period.

3 The stopwatch is started and the participant sprints to the cone marked B and touches the bottom of the cone with their right hand.

4 They then use side steps to move to cone C and touch the bottom of the cone with their left hand.

5 They then use side steps to move to cone D and touch the bottom of the cone with their right hand.

6 They then run backwards to cone A and the stopwatch is stopped once they are in line with cone A.

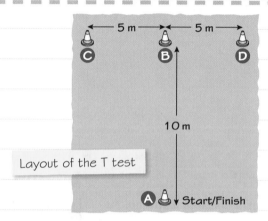

Layout of the T test

Interpreting results

Rating	Males (seconds)	Females (seconds)
Excellent	<9.5	<10.5
Good	9.5–10.5	10.5–11.5
Average	10.5–11.5	11.5–12.5
Poor	>11.5	>12.5

Normative data for the T test (ages 16–19)

Reliability, validity and practicality

Reliability	Validity
• Motivation will affect reliability • Environmental conditions do not affect reliability: carried out indoors • Conditions of test environment must be the same each time (e.g. non-slip surface, distance between cones) • Administrator does not need experience.	👍 High levels for sports that require dodging movements, e.g. badminton, tennis, rugby.
	Practicality
	👍 Requires minimal equipment 👍 Easy to set up 👎 Only one person can take the test at a time 👎 Requires a helper to administer the test.

Now try this

1 Explain why the T test may be a more valid test for a tennis player to measure their agility compared to the Illinois agility run test.

2 Clara performs the T test. Her result is 11.8 seconds. What is her rating?

Think about the movements a tennis player performs when playing a game of tennis and then compare this to the types of movements included in the T test and Illinois agility run test.

Fitness tests for balance: stork stand test

Balance is the ability to maintain an upright position and is used in many different sports. This test measures **static balance**, which is the ability to remain in an upright position while stationary.

Characteristics

- Measures: static balance while standing on one leg.
- Units: seconds (s).
- Equipment: stopwatch, flat non-slip surface, paper and pen and a person to administer the test.
- Used by: gymnasts, martial arts.

Conducting the stork stand test.

Test protocol

1 The participant removes their shoes.

2 Hands are placed on hips and the person stands up straight.

3 One foot is taken off the floor and placed against the inside knee of the leg that they are standing on.

4 The participant is given one minute to practise holding this position

5 The participant then raises their heel off the floor on the leg that they are standing on and balances on the ball of their foot.

6 The stopwatch is started and the participant holds the position for as long as possible.

7 The stopwatch is stopped if:
- the supporting foot moves in any direction
- the non-supporting foot loses contact with the knee
- the heel of the supporting foot touches the floor
- hands are moved away from the hips.

8 The best of three attempts is the final score for this test.

Interpreting results

Rating	Score (seconds)
Excellent	>50
Good	40–50
Average	25–39
Fair	10–24
Poor	<10

Normative data table of stork stand test results for men and women aged 16–19

Reliability, validity and practicality

Reliability	Validity
• Motivation will not affect reliability • Environmental conditions do not affect reliability: carried out indoors. • Conditions of test environment must be the same each time (e.g. surface) • Correct technique must be maintained.	👍 High levels for sports that require an ability to balance.

Practicality	
👍 No equipment required	👍 Easy to set up
👎 Only one person can take the test at a time	👎 Requires a helper.

Now try this

Venkat takes part in the stork stand test and is able to hold the position for 42 seconds.

Identify the rating Venkat would receive for this test result.

Check the normative data table to work out what rating this person would achieve.

Fitness tests for balance: Y balance test

This balance test measures **dynamic balance**. This is the ability to remain balanced while in motion or when changing positions – for example, a gymnast requires dynamic balance when they are performing a cartwheel.

Characteristics

- Measures: ability to balance on one leg.
- Units: centimetres (cm).
- Equipment: Y balance testing equipment, tape measure, pen, paper, person to administer the test.
- Used by: gymnasts, martial artists, some team sports.

Conducting the Y balance test.

Test protocol

1 The participant removes their shoes.

2 They are permitted a trial run at performing each move on the Y balance test equipment.

3 They stand on the starting position on one foot; the other foot is placed just behind the supporting foot.

4 The non-supporting foot is moved along one of the Y balance test locations and pushes the reach indicator as far as possible while maintaining balance on the supporting leg.

5 They repeat this movement three times and the distance moved by the indicator is measured to the nearest 0.5 cm. The highest score is taken.

6 This foot is then returned to the starting position and is taken along another of the Y balance test locations.

7 The test is repeated until the non-supporting foot has completed each of the three sections of test equipment.

8 The participant must not touch their non-supporting foot down onto the floor or put their foot on top of the reach indicators.

Interpreting results

The results for this test are specific to the individual as limb length has to be taken into account – a person with longer limbs will achieve a higher score than someone with shorter limbs as they are able to move the indicator further, but this does not show that they have higher levels of balance.

Reliability, validity and practicality

Reliability	Validity
• Motivation will affect reliability	👍 High for sports where the participant must remain balanced while performing movements
• Environmental conditions do not affect reliability: carried out indoors	👍 Can help to check if the person needs to improve other components of fitness such as strength and flexibility, which are required to help improve balance.
• Conditions of test environment must be the same each time (e.g. surface)	**Practicality**
• The way the reach indicator is pushed by the foot should be the same for each test; ensure the participant doesn't kick the indicators, making them travel further	👎 Requires specialist equipment
• The administrator needs some experience.	👎 Requires a person to administer the test
	👎 Only one person at a time can take the test.

Now try this

How are the reach indicators set out in the Y balance test?

Fitness tests for coordination: alternate-hand wall-toss test

This test measures hand–eye coordination to test how the information the participant receives from their eyes controls their ability to direct their hands to catch a ball.

Characteristics

- Measures: hand–eye coordination.
- Units: catches per 30 seconds.
- Equipment: tennis ball, stopwatch, wall, measuring tape, pen, paper, person to administer the test.
- Used by: cricket, rounders, badminton players.

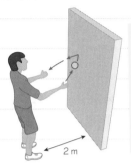

2 m

If the person throws the ball with a lot of force or not in a straight line it will affect their ability to catch it, so it is important that they throw the ball in the same way throughout the test.

Test protocol

1. The participant carries out a warm-up.

2. A line is marked out 2 m from the wall. The participant stands behind this line facing the wall.

3. The assistant starts the stopwatch and tells the participant to start.

4. The participant throws the tennis ball underarm against the wall using their right hand and catches it with their left hand.

5. They then throw the ball with their left hand against the wall and catch it with their right hand.

1. This process is repeated for 30 seconds.

2. The assistant counts the number of catches in this time period.

3. The test is stopped after 30 seconds and number of catches recorded.

Interpreting results

Age	Excellent	Above average	Average	Below average	Poor
15–16 years	>35	30–35	25–29	20–24	<20

Interpretation of alternate-hand wall-toss test results for 15–16-year-olds

Reliability, validity and practicality

Reliability	Validity
• Motivation will not affect reliability • Environmental conditions do not affect reliability: carried out indoors • Conditions of test environment must be the same each time (e.g. surface) • Standardised test procedures: throw the ball the same way throughout the test • Administrator does not need experience. • Marking a target on the wall to aim for will increase reliability.	👍 High levels for sports that require hand–eye coordination, e.g. basketball, cricket.
	Practicality
	👍 Requires minimal equipment 👍 Easy to set up 👎 Requires a person to administer the test 👎 Only one person can take the test at a time.

Now try this

Sasha is a cricket player. She conducts the alternate-hand wall-toss test. She catches 26 balls in 30 seconds.

Check the normative data table to help you.

Identify the rating Sasha would receive for this test result.

Fitness tests for coordination: stick flip coordination test

This test measures hand–eye coordination. The protocol is split into two parts: the half flip and the full flip. The participant is given three practice attempts before each part of the test.

Characteristics

- Measures: hand–eye coordination.
- Equipment: stick flip test equipment – three sticks each 60 cm long, 2 cm wide with tape at one end. Pen and paper and person to administer the test.
- Used by: badminton, squash players.

Half flip test protocol

1 The participant holds a stick in each hand. Upper arms are held at the side of the body, elbows flexed and hands held at waist height.

2 The assistant places the third stick across the two sticks held by the participant.

3 The participant tries to flip the balanced stick so that it rotates and lands back on to the balanced sticks.

4 Five flips should be attempted with each successful attempt recorded. One point per successful flip.

5 If the stick does not rotate or is dropped it is not counted.

Full flip test protocol

1 Start in the same starting position as with the half flip.

2 The participant has to perform a full flip with the balanced stick. This can be shown with the tape at the end of the stick returning to its initial side of the balanced sticks.

3 Five full flips should be attempted.

4 Each full flip is recorded and awarded 2 points.

5 If the stick does not rotate or is dropped it is not counted.

Add up the scores for the two tests to arrive at the final result.

Interpreting results

Rating	Males	Females
Excellent	14–15	13–15
Very good	11–13	10–12
Fair	5–10	4–9
Poor	3–4	2–3
Very poor	0–2	0–1

Normative data for males and females, number of successful flips per five attempts

Reliability, validity and practicality

Reliability	Validity
• Motivation will not affect reliability • Environmental conditions do not affect reliability: carried out indoors • Administrator does not need experience. • Ensure the participant practises three times. Increase in performance can come with practice rather than an increase in coordination levels.	👎 Tests hand–eye coordination but has minimal replication of movements performed in sport.
	Practicality
	👍 Easy to set up 👎 Requires specific equipment 👎 Only one person can take the test at a time 👎 Requires a helper to administer.

Now try this

Sam takes part in the stick flip test. He is not given the opportunity to carry out the three practice tests.

How might this affect the reliability of the test results?

Reliability is the repeatability of the test results. If the person were to perform the test again, are they likely to get the same results?

Fitness tests for power: vertical jump test

Power is a combination of strength and speed and is used in sports for explosive movements such as jumping high, throwing or sprinting.

Characteristics

- Measures: power in the legs.
- Units: height in cm.
- Equipment: wall, measuring tape/rule or vertical jump board, pen and paper, person to administer the test.
- Used by: high jump, basketball, netball.

Performing the vertical jump test

Test protocol

1 Perform a short warm-up before starting.

2 Stand with your dominant side against the board or wall, feet together and reach up as high as possible to record your standing reach height.

3 Make the jump and touch the vertical jump board or wall at the peak of your jump. (If using a wall, hold a tape or rule against the wall to measure the distance jumped.)

4 Only one dip of the arms and knees is permitted.

5 Perform three attempts with a rest in between each.

6 The best of three attempts is recorded.

Interpreting results

Sex	Excellent	Above average	Average	Below average	Poor
Male	>65 cm	50–65 cm	40–49 cm	30–39 cm	<30 cm
Female	>58 cm	47–58 cm	36–46 cm	26–35 cm	<26 cm

Normative vertical jump test results for 16–19-year-olds

Reliability, validity and practicality

Reliability	Validity
• Motivation will affect reliability • Environmental conditions do not affect reliability: carried out indoors • Conditions of test environment must be the same each time (e.g. surface, measuring method) • Standardised test procedures: preparation, jump technique must be the same for each test • Administrator does not need experience.	👍 High levels for sports that require power in the legs, e.g. high jump, basketball.
	Practicality
	👍 No specialist equipment 👍 Easy to set up 👎 Only one person can take the test at a time 👎 Requires a helper to administer the test.

Now try this

1 Tomas takes part in the high jump event.
   Why do you think the vertical jump test is an appropriate test for a high jumper?

2 Isaak completes the vertical jump test. His best score is 53 cm. What is his test result?

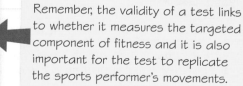

Remember, the validity of a test links to whether it measures the targeted component of fitness and it is also important for the test to replicate the sports performer's movements.

Fitness tests for power: standing long/broad jump

This test is called either the standing long jump or the broad jump. While the names may differ, the test protocol and normative data remain the same.

Characteristics

- Measures: power in the legs.
- Units: centimetres (cm).
- Equipment: measuring tape, marking tape/chalk, pen and paper and person to administer the test.
- Used by: long jump, basketball.

Performing the standing long jump

Test protocol

1 Perform a short warm-up before starting.

2 Stand behind a line marked on the ground.

3 Feet should be hip distance apart. The participant pushes down on both feet, swings their arms and bends their knees and jumps as far forward as possible.

4 The participant must land on both feet and try not to fall backwards.

5 The distance is measured from the take-off line to the nearest point of contact to the take-off line (back of the heels).

6 The test is repeated three times with a rest period between each attempt.

7 The longest distance recorded is the score recorded.

Interpreting results

Rating	Males (cm)	Females (cm)
Excellent	>244	>191
Above average	229–244	178–191
Average	216–228	163–177
Below average	198–215	150–162
Poor	<198	<150

Normative data for the standing long jump for men and women aged 16+ (in cm)

Reliability, validity and practicality

Reliability	Validity
<ul><li>Motivation will affect reliability</li><li>Environmental conditions may affect reliability if conducted outdoors</li><li>Conditions of test environment must be the same each time (e.g. surface, measuring method)</li><li>Standardised test procedures: warm-up, preparation, technique, follow-through movement must be the same for each test</li><li>Administrator does not need experience.</li></ul>	👍 High levels for sports that require power in the legs, e.g. long jump, hurdles, netball.
	Practicality
	👍 No specialist equipment
	👍 Easy to set up
	👎 Only one person can take the test at a time
	👎 Requires a helper to administer.

Now try this

Janice is a netball player and plays in the position of goalkeeper.

Explain **one** reason why the standing broad jump would be a more valid test for a netballer than a baseball player.

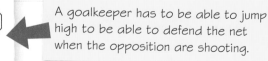

A goalkeeper has to be able to jump high to be able to defend the net when the opposition are shooting.

Fitness tests for power: Margaria-Kalamen power test

This test takes into account a person's weight and provides an overall score of power in their legs.

Characteristics

- Measures: power in the legs.
- Units: watts.
- Equipment: stopwatch, flight of steps (12 steps, 17.5 cm high), weighing scales, cones for marking, pen and paper and person to administer the test.
- Used by: high jump, long jump, sprinting.

Performing the Margaria-Kalamen test

Test protocol

1 A cone is placed on the 3rd, 6th and 9th step.

2 The vertical distance is measured between the 3rd and 9th step in metres.

3 The participant is weighed (kg) and the results recorded.

4 The participant performs a short warm-up.

5 The participant stands 6 m from the first step.

6 The assistant says 'go'.

7 The participant sprints to and up the stairs, at a time landing on the 3rd, 6th and 9th step.

8 The assistant starts the stopwatch when the participant's foot lands on the 3rd step and stops it when their foot lands on the 9th step.

9 This time is recorded.

Interpreting results

There are no normative data tables for this test. However, it can be used to compare test results to check if a power training programme is helping to increase power in the legs.

Power (watts) is calculated by using the following formula:

$$P = (M \times D) \times \frac{9.8}{t}$$

P = power (watts)
M = athlete's weight (kg)
D = vertical distance (m) from 3rd to 9th step
t = time

 Real world **Example**

Jim weighs 70 kg. The vertical distance between the 3rd and 9th step is 1 m. He completes the test in 2 seconds. His result is:

$$P \text{ (watts)} = (70 \times 1) \times \frac{9.8}{2} = 343 \text{ watts}$$

Reliability, validity and practicality

Reliability	Validity
• Motivation will affect reliability • Environmental conditions do not affect reliability: usually carried out indoors • Conditions of test environment must be the same each time (e.g. measuring method) • Assistant must start and stop the stopwatch at the right times • Reliability improved if a timing mat is used • Administrator does not need experience.	👍 High validity for sports that require power in the legs, e.g. sprinting, football, hurdling.

Validity
👍 High validity for sports that require power in the legs, e.g. sprinting, football, hurdling.

Practicality
👍 Requires minimal equipment
👍 Easy to set up
👎 Only one person can take the test at a time
👎 Requires a helper to administer.

Now try this

Explain **one** reason why a hurdler would use the Margaria-Kalamen power test to assess their fitness for hurdling.

How would this component of fitness be used in a hurdling race?

Fitness tests for reaction time: ruler drop test

This test measures how quickly a person is able to respond and catch a falling ruler.

Characteristics

- Measures: reaction time.
- Units: centimetres (cm).
- Equipment: metre rule.
- Used by: sprinters, footballers, badminton and table tennis players.

Performing the ruler drop test

Test protocol

1 The metre rule is held by the person administering the test.

2 The participant holds their hand out with their index finger and thumb of their dominant hand around the ruler so that the top of their thumb is level with the 0 line on the 1-metre rule.

3 The assistant releases the ruler and the participant has to catch it as soon as possible.

4 The distance between the top of the thumb where the participant has caught the ruler and bottom of the ruler is measured.

5 The test is carried out three times and an average value is used for the overall test result.

Interpreting results

Excellent	Above average	Average	Below average	Poor
<7.5cm	7.5–15.9cm	15.9–20.4cm	20.4–28cm	>28cm

Normative data for the ruler drop test (in cm)

Online reaction time test and reaction test timer

There are other methods of testing reaction time using specific computer apps or a timer. The computer app or test timer will ask a participant to respond to key information in a given way as quickly as possible and record how long it takes for the reaction time of that person.

Reliability, validity and practicality

Reliability	Validity
• Motivation will not affect reliability • Environmental conditions do not affect reliability: carried out indoors • Assistant must take a consistent approach on how they drop the ruler. Any force imparted when it is dropped could affect the rate of fall • Assistant must accurately line up the bottom of the ruler with the finger and thumb.	👍 Valid for overall reaction rate for how quickly a person responds to a stimulus. Useful for sports such as badminton, volleyball, table tennis.
	Practicality
	👍 No specialist equipment 👍 Easy to set up 👎 Only one person can take the test at a time 👎 Requires a helper to administer.

Now try this

Corey takes part in the ruler drop test. He gets a score of 18.4 cm.

Identify what rating Corey would achieve from this score.

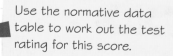

Use the normative data table to work out the test rating for this score.

Warm-up

Every training session in a fitness programme should have three components: a warm-up, the main activity or activities and a cool down. A coach will need to be able to plan appropriate activities for each of these components.

Why warm up?

A warm-up is important to prepare the body for exercise. It increases:

- heart and breathing rates
- the temperature of the muscles
- the range of movement available at the joints and muscles.

There are three components to a warm-up: pulse raiser, mobiliser and stretch.

Avoiding injury

If you don't warm up properly before taking part in exercise, the muscles and ligaments will not be warm enough to allow them to stretch to the degree needed to perform sport or physical activity.

This puts you at greater risk of picking up injuries such as a muscle strain or a ligament sprain.

It is important to make sure that the activities carried out in the warm-up properly prepare the person for the type of training and component(s) of fitness being trained.

① Pulse raiser

This is the first part of a warm-up. The pulse raiser increases blood flow around the body:

- The contracting of the muscles during the pulse raiser generates heat, which warms up the blood.
- This increases the temperature of the body.

There should be a progressive increase in the intensity of pulse raiser activities, for example from a brisk walk to a slow jog then to a faster jog. Games that gradually increase pulse rate can also be included in the pulse raiser.

② Mobiliser

The second part of the warm-up mobilises the joints of the body, ready for participation in sport and physical activity.

This process increases the production of synovial fluid in the joints:

- This helps the bones that meet at the joint to slide over each other more easily, and increases the range of movement available at the joint.

The main joints of the body include the knees, hips, shoulders, ankles and wrists.

Examples of movements in the mobiliser include: circling actions of the joint such as bent arm and straight arm shoulder circles, hip circles, etc.

③ Stretch

The main muscles that are going to be used in the sport or physical activity should be stretched during the last part of the warm-up. Static active stretches and static passive stretches can be used:

- **Static active stretches** – the person and stretches for a short period of time and holds the position themselves.
- **Static passive stretches** – uses another person or object to hold the correct position while the stretch is held for a short period of time.

Revise static stretches on page 48.

Duration of warm-up

Around 5–10 minutes is usually enough for the warm-up, but the exact duration will depend on a variety of factors.

In cold conditions, more time will be needed for the warm-up, as it will take longer to increase the temperature of the body.

People who are new to exercising will need longer, as more time is needed to:

- teach the correct techniques for each part of the warm-up
- ensure that the participant carries out the movements safely and in a controlled manner.

Now try this

Name **two** components of a warm-up.

 A component is a section of the warm-up. A warm-up has three components, but you only need to include two in your answer here.

Cool down

The final component in any fitness programme is cooling down. You must remember to include a cool down activity that is appropriate for the type of activity that the participant has done.

Why cool down?

 1 Cooling down returns the body to its pre-exercise state by gradually decreasing the pulse and breathing rate.

 2 It helps to remove the waste products such as lactic acid produced during exercise.

 3 The cool down is necessary for maintaining flexibility.

The cool down activities should take into account the type of training that a person has taken part in such as the main muscles involved to ensure they are fully stretched.

Components of a cool down

There are two components in a cool down:

1 **Pulse lowering**

Activities are required that gradually decrease in intensity and lower the pulse and breathing rate.

- Taking part in an active cool down helps to remove lactic acid at a faster rate than just stopping exercise.
- This means you are less likely to suffer from muscle soreness.
- Pulse lowering could involve slowing down from a run to a gentle jog, then to a fast walk and finally a slower walk.

2 **Stretch**

This involves **maintenance** and **developmental** stretches of the main muscles that were used in the activity session.

- Once you stop exercising, the muscles can remain in a slightly contracted state – a little shorter than before taking part in the exercise.
- This will eventually result in a decrease in flexibility and an increased risk of straining a muscle.
- Stretches are used in the cool down to return the working muscles to their resting length.

Types of stretching in a cool down

Maintenance and developmental stretches of different muscles are carried out in a cool down. See the table below.

Maintenance stretches are held for 15 seconds. They are used to maintain the length of a muscle rather than lengthen it.

This type of stretch is used for muscles where increased flexibility is not usually beneficial to sporting performance.

Developmental stretches are held for longer, usually around 30 seconds, to help lengthen the muscle and increase flexibility.

Maintenance	Developmental
• Deltoids	• Hip flexors
• Triceps	• Hamstrings
• Gastrocnemius	• Gluteus maximus
• Quadriceps	• Erector spinae
• Obliques	
• Abdominals	
• Biceps	

 Now try this

Identify an activity that a person could take part in to lower their pulse and reduce their breathing rate.

To lower pulse rate the activity should decrease in intensity.

Fitness training methods for aerobic endurance

Appropriate training methods can be used to improve aerobic endurance levels for a specific sport or activity.

Principles of aerobic training

Aerobic training aims to improve the efficiency of the cardiorespiratory system so that more oxygen and nutrients are delivered to the working muscles and more waste products are removed. This allows the participant to take part in their sport for longer periods of time at the same intensity.

This type of training can take place indoors or outdoors, although the weather can impact performance if outdoors.

> You need to apply the FITT and Additional principles of training to each training method (pages 2–6 and 7–14).

1 Interval training

Interval training involves exercising at 60–80% Max HR followed by a recovery period.

- The time spent exercising can vary from a few seconds to many minutes.
- The recovery period may involve complete rest or exercising at very low intensity.
- To develop aerobic endurance, the length of the rest periods should be decreased and the exercise periods increased.

Advantages

👍 Interval training replicates a range of sports involving rest periods – netball players walk back to their positions after a team has scored.

👎 With all aerobic endurance training you must have enough time for at least 30 minutes' regular training.

2 Continuous training

Continuous training involves exercising at a constant moderate intensity for at least 30 minutes. It can include jogging, swimming and cycling. The participant's heart rate (HR) should remain at 60–80% of their maximum. Revise intensity of training on page 4.

Advantages and disadvantages

👍 Good for sports where a person exercises for long periods of time at the same intensity, such as a 10 km flat race

👍 Does not replicate the type of fitness needed for many sports, when the exercise intensity varies and the heart rate may go above 80% max

👎 Can become tedious.

3 Fartlek training

Continuous moderate training is combined with higher-intensity exercise.

- For example, swimming at a set pace of 60–80% Max HR, then sprinting a few lengths beyond 80% Max HR.
- Intensity can also be increased by using resistance, such as running uphill or with a weighted backpack.
- There are no rest periods in fartlek training.

Advantages and disadvantages

👍 Helps to develop speed during the higher-intensity training, and aerobic endurance during the moderate-intensity training

👍 Prepares participants for sports that combine continuous moderate intensity with higher-intensity exercise, such as football

👎 Can be difficult to measure.

4 Circuit training

Circuit training uses a number of stations with different exercises completed in succession, with minimal rest periods. The stations should challenge the cardiovascular system. Step ups, shuttle runs and skipping would all be appropriate stations to develop aerobic endurance.

Advantages and disadvantages

👍 Stations can be sport-specific and add variety

👎 Can take time to set up.

Now try this

Explain **one** way a cross-country runner could increase the intensity of their fartlek training.

Fitness training methods for flexibility

Flexibility training plays an important part in injury prevention and is beneficial for sporting performance. Participants whose joints can move through their full range of movement are more able to perform specific sporting techniques correctly. Look back at the flexibility tests on pages 26–28.

Methods of improving flexibility include static active stretching, static passive stretching and proprioceptive neuromuscular facilitation (PNF) stretching.

> You need to apply the FITT and additional principles of training to each training method. Look back at pages 2–6 and 7–12 to remind yourself how to do this.

Static active stretching

The participant gets into a specific position to target a specific muscle or muscle group and holds the position to develop the stretch.

> Static active stretching is done using your own body. The stretch needs to be held for 12–30 seconds.

Static passive stretching

Static passive stretching involves another person or object to hold the body part being stretched in the correct position.

> A static passive stretch is also held for 12–30 seconds.

Advantages and disadvantages

👍 Useful for almost all sports as helps to increase flexibility in specific areas of the body required for particular sports

👍 As with all types of stretching, little or no equipment is needed so there are no costs and no time required setting up equipment

👍 There is no limit to how many people can take part.

👎 It can take some time to fully develop flexibility in targeted areas

👎 High levels of motivation are needed to carry out exercises regularly

👎 A coach/instructor may be needed to advise on correct technique, as there can be a risk of injury if stretches are not performed correctly.

Proprioceptive neuromuscular facilitation (PNF) stretching

PNF stretching requires a partner to provide resistance.

1 The participant stretches the muscle or muscle group as far as possible.

2 The partner holds the body part being stretched while the participant pushes against their partner for 6–10 seconds.

3 The participant then relaxes the muscle while the partner pushes the body part to increase the stretch.

The process is repeated about three times.

Advantages and disadvantages

👍 It helps to develop flexibility at a faster rate than other types of flexibility training.

👍 No equipment needed, so no costs nor time spent having to set up equipment.

👎 Cannot be performed individually, so needs another person to carry out the stretching process.

👎 There is a risk of injury if the stretching partner lacks experience.

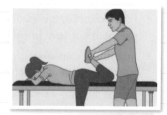

A PNF stretch for the quadriceps

Now try this

Jan is a gymnast. She wants to increase her flexibility as quickly as possible in preparation for a gymnastics event in six weeks' time.

Which method of flexibility training would be most suitable for Jan?

Fitness training methods for muscular endurance

Muscular endurance is usually needed in sports and activities where high levels of aerobic endurance are also required. Look back at the muscular endurance fitness tests on pages 23–25.

Principles of muscular endurance training

Muscular endurance training increases the ability of the trained muscles to contract repeatedly for long periods of time. Training should include:

- a high number of repetitions (reps)
- low resistance or load.

Examples

- When performing bicep curls, three sets of 15 reps using a weight of 5 kg could be used.
- Cycling is also an example of muscular endurance for legs because it involves pushing down on the pedals many times (high reps) and the resistance is relatively low (low weights).

Circuit training

This involves stations of muscular endurance exercises arranged in a circuit. Participants carry out each exercise for a period of time before moving on to the next one. Short rest periods can be included between each station.

Advantages and disadvantages

👍 It can be tailored to a specific sport, with drills from the sport included.

👍 Different muscle groups are exercised at each station to improve whole body muscular endurance.

👍 The stations can be changed at each training session to avoid boredom.

👍 It is usually a group exercise, which can help with motivation.

👎 It takes time to set out the circuit with appropriate equipment and labels.

Remember to apply the FITT and additional principles of training to each training method.

Free weights and fixed resistance machines

Fixed weights and free weights can be used to carry out muscular endurance training.

- Fixed weights are part of resistance machines that only permit certain movements.
- Free weights are barbells, dumbbells and kettle bells, which can be used for different types of exercises.

Advantages and disadvantages

Free weights:

👍 can be used for different types of exercises and different muscle groups.

👍 can be used in a group session.

👎 have a risk of injury from over-extending joints.

Resistance machines:

👍 are useful for targeting specific muscle groups.

👍 have a lower risk of injury.

👎 are specialised and usually only available in a gym.

👎 can only be used by one person at a time.

👎 a helper should monitor the use of free weights and sometimes resistance machines if the user is inexperienced.

Body resistance exercises in circuit training

Body weight resistance exercises can be used to provide appropriate resistance for muscular endurance, using low loads and high repetitions.

Exercise	Muscle group targeted
Sit-ups	Abdominals
Triceps dips	Triceps
Lunges/squats	Quadriceps and gluteals
Press-ups	Pectorals and triceps

Now try this

How should weights be used in a circuit to develop muscular endurance?

 Think about the number of reps and the load.

Fitness training methods for muscular strength

The purpose of strength training is to increase the size of a person's muscles. The larger the muscles, the more force they can exert and the more strength they have. Look back at page 30–31 to revise strength tests.

Principles of strength training

To increase strength, muscle tissue needs to be overloaded using heavy weights to cause muscle **hypertrophy** (an increase in muscle size). Strength training exercises involve carrying out low numbers of reps using high loads (heavy weights). This is the opposite to training for muscular endurance. Free weights and resistance machines can also be used to help increase muscle size and improve a person's strength.

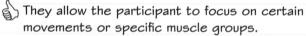

Free weights

A free weight is one that is not attached to machinery.

- A dumbbell is a short bar with a weight at each end, used with one in each hand.
- A barbell is a longer bar with a weight at each end, used with both hands.

Dumbbells are available in different weights to suit different levels of strength and to allow for progression.

Advantages

👍 Free weight training increases strength over a large range of movements.

👍 They allow the participant to focus on certain movements or specific muscle groups.

👍 Targeting specific muscle groups helps increase strength for particular sports.

👍 Free weights can be stored and used at home.

👍 The same equipment can be used to train different muscle groups.

Disadvantages

👎 Weight training exercises rarely replicate the movements carried out in sport fully – although muscle size will increase, the range of movement actually used in sport might not.

👎 Training cannot be carried out alone – a spotter is needed to ensure the participant's safety.

👎 To ensure the participant's safety, training should not be carried out when fatigued. This can increase the chance of not being able to lift the weight and incurring injuries.

👎 They can be expensive to buy if training at home.

Fixed resistance machines

Resistance machines use stacks of weights attached to pulleys or air pressure to provide resistance.

Each machine is designed to perform one type of strength training exercise, and so only permits specific movement patterns to train specific muscles or groups of muscles.

> You need to apply the FITT and Additional principles of training to each training method. Look back at pages 2–6 and 7–12 to remind yourself how to do this.

Advantages and disadvantages

👍 They can increase the strength of targeted muscles and muscle groups for particular sports.

👍 They are safer than free weights for people new to weight training – there is less chance of injury from not being able to lift the weight.

👍 Participants can train alone.

👎 The equipment is expensive.

👎 You might need to join a gym or leisure centre to use the equipment.

👎 Each machine usually exercises only one muscle or muscle group, so many different pieces of equipment are required.

Now try this

Molly wants to improve her strength but has never carried out any strength training before.

Which method of strength training would you recommend for Molly?

Which type of equipment is easiest and safest for a person who is new to strength training?

Fitness training methods for speed

Speed is important for athletic track events and sprint cycling, as well as in team games (such as sprinting to intercept a ball or get ahead of an opponent). There are different types of speed training including interval training, acceleration sprint training and resistance drills. Revise the speed training fitness tests on page 29.

Interval training

- For interval training that aims to develop speed, very short, high-intensity work periods are followed by a rest or recovery period.
- Speed is developed by increasing work intensity and decreasing the number of rest periods.
- Intervals will vary depending on the athlete's goals.

Advantages and disadvantages

👍 Good for sports that have varied intensity with recovery periods, e.g. rugby, basketball, football

👍 No equipment needed

👍 No training facility required

👍 Can involve a number of participants at the same time

👎 Does not always replicate sport specific movements

👎 High-intensity exercise can increase the risk of injury.

Resistance drills

- Resistance can be used to increase the load the participant has to sprint against. This overloads the muscles to make them stronger.
- Bungee ropes, resistance bands, sleds or a parachute can provide increased load.
- Running uphill can also provide resistance. This increases the intensity of the sprinting, overloading the sprinting muscles.
- Assisted sprinting, such as running downhill, makes sprinting easier and helps the muscles get used to the process of moving at speed.

Advantages and disadvantages

👍 Good for sports that involve travelling at speed, e.g. hockey, basketball

👍 Good for sports that require sprinting in a straight line, e.g. 100 m sprint

👍 Equipment can be used to add resistance and variety

👎 Equipment is specialist and can be expensive

👎 Only useful for sports that include sprinting in one direction

👎 Risk of injury can be increased if not warmed up properly.

Resistance can be provided by using bungee ropes, a parachute or sprinting uphill.

Remember to apply the FITT and additional principles of training to each training method.

Acceleration sprints

- Acceleration sprints replicate the type of sprinting that takes place in many different sports such as netball when a player is jogging to receive a pass and then increases their speed to sprint with the ball to run past defenders.
- Pace is gradually increased from a standing or rolling start to jogging, then to striding and then to a maximal sprint.
- Rest intervals of jogging or walking are used between each repetition.

Advantages and disadvantages

👍 Good form of aerobic training

👍 No equipment needed

👍 No training facility required

👍 Can be done by a number of participants at the same time

👍 Intensity is gradually increased so risk of injury is reduced

👎 Only useful for sports that include sprinting in one direction.

Now try this

Suggest **one** training method a rugby player could use to improve speed and explain why.

 Think about what type of speed is needed in rugby.

Fitness training methods for agility, coordination and reaction time

Agility, coordination and reaction time can be trained to improve performance in sports where high levels of these components are required. Revise the fitness tests on pages 35–36, 39–40 and 44.

Speed, agility and quickness (SAQ) training

Agility is important in sports that require a person to change direction quickly and still maintain their balance.

For this type of training, SAQ equipment or training principles are used. This method involves sprinting and then changing direction over a set course, which is designed to replicate sport-specific speed requirements.

Advantages and disadvantages

👍 Can be made sport specific

👍 Suitable for all ages and abilities

👍 Good for sports that include a change of direction when sprinting, such as rugby or hockey

👍 Equipment is cheap, easy to use and adds variety, which helps prevent boredom

👎 Time is needed to set up the equipment prior to the training.

👎 Requires specialised training equipment

👎 Requires relatively high fitness levels so the participant doesn't get too tired and injure themselves from poor technique.

Coordination training

Coordination is the ability to use two or more parts of the body smoothly and efficiently at the same time. It can include using sports equipment.

- Most sports will have sport-specific coordination training where the type of movement required in that sport is trained for, such as performing a cartwheel in gymnastics.

- Hand–eye coordination can also be trained, for example coordinating the arm to move a racquet at the right time to hit a tennis ball.

- Other examples are skipping, dribbling, juggling.

This type of training should be carried out towards the start of a training session before the person is too tired to focus on the motor skills required.

Advantages and disadvantages

👍 Can be made sport specific

👍 Does not require specialised training equipment

👎 Can lead to injury (such as falling or straining a muscle) if the person loses concentration.

> Remember to apply the FITT and Additional principles of training to each training method. Look back at pages 2–6 and 7–12 to remind yourself how to do this

Reaction time training

Reaction time is the ability to respond quickly to an external stimulus.

- This type of training is usually sport specific.

- For example, a sprinter needs to be able to respond quickly to the starter's pistol so that they can get up and out of the blocks quickly to get ahead of the other sprinters.

Advantages and disadvantages

👍 Can be made sport specific

👎 As the person has to complete a response very quickly, they must be fully warmed up to avoid injury

👎 May require specialised training equipment.

Examples

- A coach signals for a sprinter to start at irregular timings

- Cross-country/uneven terrain running – this helps to learn how to react quickly to obstacles

- Interactive light boards.

Now try this

Describe a method of training that would help to improve a sprint swimmer's reaction time for 50 m swimming races.

> The training should replicate the requirements of the sport in order for it to be effective.

Fitness training methods for power

Power training involves using lower weights (loads) or resistance than strength training, and the types of exercises carried out allow the participant to perform a high number of repetitions. This simulates repeated use of power in sports such as the shot put, basketball and gymnastics. Revise the power training fitness tests on pages 41–43. Plyometrics is a training method for improving power.

Plyometrics

Plyometric training involves making a muscle produce its maximum force in the fastest possible time.

- It uses movements that lengthen the muscle and then immediately shorten it, such as jumping on and off benches or over bars to develop power in the legs.
- The shorter the time between the lengthening and shortening of the muscle, the more power is generated.
- Intensity can be carefully increased by increasing the number of repetitions of an exercise.
- Exercises need to be performed on a suitable surface that will absorb some of the force being produced.

This type of training is of a high intensity and should only be used after a thorough warm-up and with participants that have high fitness levels to avoid the risk of injury.

Advantages and disadvantages

👍 Can be targeted for the muscle groups that require power

👍 Equipment usually consists of benches or boxes, which are cheap and relatively easy to set up

👍 Can be performed alone and at times to suit the individual

👎 Equipment needs to be set up prior to training

👎 Can cause injury as the muscles have to withstand high levels of stress

👎 This training is intense and can result in injury

👎 Not suitable for young athletes.

Examples of plyometric exercises

Which type of plyometric training is best will depend on which muscle groups are required for the participant's sport.

Sports that require high levels of power in the leg and lower body muscles would benefit from:

- jumping on and off benches
- jumping lunges
- bounding
- barrier hopping
- jumping.

Sports that require high levels of power in the upper body muscles would benefit from:

- throwing a medicine ball
- press ups with a clap
- incline press-up.

Suitable sports

Sports performers that benefit from plyometric training are:

- Sprinters – they need explosive power at take-off when they hear the starting gun.
- Hurdlers – they need to jump over hurdles while maintaining speed.
- Volleyball players – they need to jump high and contest the ball.
- Basketball players – need to jump as high off the ground as possible to get close to the basket.

You need to apply the FITT and additional principles of training to each training method. Look back at pages 2–6 and 7–12 to remind yourself how to do this.

Now try this

Keanu takes part in the 400 m hurdle race.

Describe what type of power training would help to improve Keanu's hurdling performance.

The type of training should replicate what is required to be able to leap over the hurdles.

53

Fitness training methods for balance

Balance is the ability of the performer to maintain their centre of mass over a base of support. There are two main types of balance that a person needs in sport: static balance and dynamic balance. Revise the fitness tests for balance on pages 37–38.

Static balance training

Static balance is the ability to remain upright when stationary:

- Training will usually involve reducing the size of the base of support such as standing on one leg or standing on the ball of one foot.
- Once effective, this should progress to dynamic balance. ◀

- Sports that require this type of balance include yoga, pilates, gymnastics.

> Remember to apply the FITT and additional principles of training to each training method. Look back at pages 2–6 and 7–12 to remind yourself how to do this.

A gymnast uses static balance for a handstand

Dynamic balance training

Dynamic balance is the ability to remain upright while moving. Training requires the person to perform movements while in a balanced position. Such as:

- standing on a dynamic balance board to increase the challenge of remaining upright
- standing on one leg and flexing and extending the support knee to move the body downwards and upwards
- lunging
- single leg Romanian deadlift.

Sports that require this type of balance include martial arts and gymnasts.

> The larger the base of support, and the lower the centre of mass to the ground, the better the person's balance.

> An athlete uses dynamic balance for a karate kick. Note that the smaller the base of support, and the higher the centre of mass from the ground, the lower the person's balance.

Core strength

Being able to remain balanced requires a person to have high levels of core strength, and training to be able to control the body parts so that they can remain in a fixed position.

The core consists of the back muscles and muscles around the abdomen.

Base of support and centre of gravity

- The **base of support** is the area of ground that a person's body comes into contact with. This is usually the feet for most sports.
- The **centre of gravity** is the area in the body where the weight is evenly dispersed.

Advantages and disadvantages of balance training

👍 Suitable for all ages and abilities

👍 Any number of people can take part

👍 Can usually be done anywhere

👎 Specialist equipment can sometimes be required for dynamic balance

👎 Older people or those recovering from injury may need additional support from a trainer and physical support (such as something to hold on to) to prevent injury if they were to lose balance and fall over.

Now try this

Jan is a gymnast. To perform well on the beam she needs to have high levels of balance. ◀

How can Jan train to improve her static balance?

> A gymnastic beam is very narrow and gymnasts need to be able to perform different routines on the beam and not fall off.

Public, private and voluntary provision

Fitness training tends to be offered by a range of providers in the public, private and voluntary sectors. Each varies in terms of the equipment available, cost, support and access.

1 Public sector

This sector is funded by the government. Money is raised by charging the general public tax and then this money is invested in sport. In deprived areas, public sector provision can be essential as individuals in these communities cannot afford to access private facilities.

Disadvantages of public sector facilities

👎 Their facilities offer sports opportunities rather than comfort or luxury

👎 They may have out-of-date equipment

👎 They may not be able to offer anything other than access to training equipment with no other products or services available.

Advantages of public sector facilities

👍 They are funded by money from the local council

👍 They are large in size so can accommodate a lot of people

👍 They have low prices and concessions to allow as many people as possible to participate

👍 They offer facilities for team and individual sports.

> Examples of these types of facilities include local leisure centres and swimming pools.

2 Private sector

The private sector exists to make a profit. The organisations are privately owned and provide a level of service based on price. The more a customer pays, the better level of service and facilities they can expect.

Advantages of private sector facilities

👍 They can offer specialist services and products, such as fitness classes or sports massage therapists that clients can access as part of their membership

👍 They tend to be plush and luxurious

👍 There are often social areas for members to meet up and purchase refreshments

👍 They will usually have the latest training equipment.

Disadvantages of private sector facilities

👎 They are often expensive to join

👎 They are aimed at certain groups of people rather than the general public

👎 People have to be members and pay monthly or yearly

👎 They provide mainly for individual sports and health and fitness.

> Examples of these types of facility are private health clubs.

3 Voluntary sector

The voluntary sector is run by people who work for free. This is usually because they have a common interest in the sport or activity that they are helping out at. Volunteers may have previously participated in that sport or are related to a participant.

Advantages of voluntary sector facilities

👍 They focus on fitness for competitive sports

👍 Coaches have a lot of experience in the sport and have usually played at a high level themselves

👍 They are usually low cost to use.

Disadvantages of voluntary sector facilities

👎 They offer fitness training opportunities for only one sport

👎 Facilities and equipment can be quite basic

👎 They rarely own their own facilities and equipment so may have limited training times available.

> Examples include local junior sports teams such as football or cricket.

Now try this

Shazny is a rugby player.

Suggest **one** advantage of private provision and the benefit of this to the performer.

The effects of long-term fitness training: aerobic endurance training

Regular aerobic endurance training over a period of at least six weeks leads to adaptations of the cardiovascular and respiratory systems.

Adaptations to the cardiovascular system

The cardiovascular system consists of the heart, the blood vessels and blood. Its main function is to transport oxygen and nutrients around the body and remove waste products. Adaptations include:

Anatomy of the Human Heart

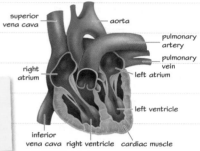

1 Cardiac hypertrophy

This is where the size of the heart muscle increases, which means the heart can contract with more force so that it can pump more blood out per beat. The amount of blood pumped out by the heart is called the **stroke volume**.

> The left ventricle increases in size the most as it has to pump blood around the body, whereas the right ventricle only has to pump to the lungs.

2 Decreased resting heart rate

Cardiac output is the amount of blood that needs to be circulated when at rest for the body to function at optimal levels. It is calculated by multiplying heart rate by stroke volume.

Cardiac output = Heart rate (HR) × Stroke volume (SV)

If stroke volume increases due to cardiac hypertrophy, the heart does not need to beat as often to produce the same cardiac output at rest.

> **Real world** **Example**
>
> If average cardiac output is 5 litres at rest, then:
>
> - an untrained person with a stroke volume of 50 ml would need to have a resting HR of 100 bpm to achieve a cardiac output of 5 l:
>   100 (HR) × 50 (SV) = 5000 ml (5 l)
>
> - a trained person with a stroke volume of 100 ml would need to have a resting HR of 50 bpm to achieve a cardiac output of 5 l:
>   50 (HR) × 100 (SV) = 5000 ml (5 l)

Adaptations to the respiratory system

The main function of the respiratory system is to bring oxygen into the body and remove carbon dioxide.

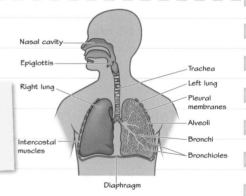

1 Increased strength of the respiratory muscles

The diaphragm and intercostal muscles increase in strength in response to aerobic endurance training. This helps a person inspire (breathe in) more air and expire (breath out) more air per breath:

- More oxygen breathed in can be used to supply energy through the aerobic energy system for muscle contraction.
- More waste products from the aerobic energy system can be breathed out.

> The respiratory system consists of the trachea, bronchi, bronchioles, alveoli, diaphragm and intercostal muscles.

2 Capillarisation around alveoli

Gaseous exchange happens in the alveoli. This means oxygen diffuses into the blood stream and carbon dioxide (a waste product), diffuses out of the blood and into the alveoli. This occurs at the capillaries which have semi-permeable membranes that allow gases to diffuse into and out of the blood carried in the capillaries.

Now try this

Explain one way the cardiovascular system adapts to aerobic endurance training to improve long-distance running performance.

> Think about how these adaptions improve running performance.

The effects of long-term fitness training: flexibility training

Taking part in flexibility training leads mainly to adaptations of the muscular and skeletal systems.

Adaptations to the muscular and skeletal systems

The muscular system includes the skeletal muscles and tendons, which attach muscle to bones. The skeletal system includes bones and ligaments.

Where two bones meet, this is called an **articulation**. It is here that ligaments attach bones together to form joints. Ligaments also provide stability in a joint to try and prevent dislocations from occurring.

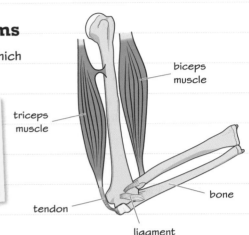

biceps muscle

triceps muscle

bone

tendon

ligament

Increased range of movement permitted at a joint

Synovial joints are the joints in the body where flexibility training can increase the range of movement permitted at the joint.

A joint is made up of a number of different components. The main components of a joint that respond to flexibility training are the ligaments, tendons and muscle tissues.

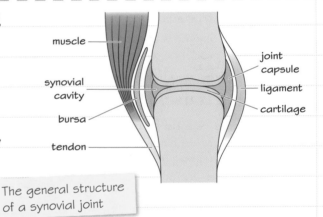

muscle

joint capsule

synovial cavity

ligament

bursa

cartilage

tendon

The general structure of a synovial joint

Increased flexibility of ligament and tendons

Flexibility training will increase the stretch permitted at ligaments and tendons. This allows the joint to have a greater range of movement.

Increased muscle length

When we take part in sport or exercise, the muscles have to contract to allow us to produce movements. However, if we don't carry out regular flexibility training, our muscles can remain slightly contracted, which reduces our flexibility.

Flexibility training helps to reset muscle tissue to its original length and can also increase the normal length of the muscle tissue to allow a person to get into positions that require high levels of flexibility such as in gymnastics.

Now try this

Why would flexibility training be beneficial for improving butterfly swimming performance?

Look at the image and work out what joint a butterfly swimmer may need high levels of flexibility in to perform well in their sport.

The effects of long-term fitness training: muscular endurance and speed training

Endurance and speed training will result in adaptations to the muscular system, such as capillarisation around muscle tissues, increased muscle tone and increased tolerance to lactic acid.

Capillarisation around muscle tissues

Muscle tissues need oxygen and nutrients, brought by blood, to provide energy through aerobic respiration. This allows them to keep contracting for long periods of time.

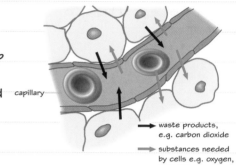

capillary

→ waste products, e.g. carbon dioxide

→ substances needed by cells e.g. oxygen, nutrients

- This occurs at the **capillaries**, which are the smallest of the blood vessels. They help to transport blood to and from the muscles.
- Capillaries have semi-permeable membranes that allow nutrients, oxygen and waste products to pass through.
- Long-term exercise can lead to an increase in the number of capillaries surrounding the muscle.
- As a result, blood flow increases.
- This allows oxygen and nutrients to be delivered more efficiently and waste products to be removed.

Capillaries surrounding muscles ensure they get the oxygen and nutrients needed to produce energy and also allow waste products to pass through.

Increased muscle tone

Muscle tone is related to how much tension our muscles have at rest, which is needed for helping us to hold our body upright when we are sitting or standing. Muscular endurance training helps to increase muscle tone, which allows us to resist movement and remain stationary.

See page 49 for more on muscular endurance training.

Muscle tone helps us to remain stationary and in an upright position.

Increased tolerance to lactic acid

Speed training also causes adaptations to the muscular system.

- Sprinting is a high-intensity activity, requiring a lot of energy to be produced at a fast rate.
- To do this, the body uses the lactic acid energy system.
- The waste product from this energy system is **lactic acid**.
- The build-up of lactic acid causes fatigue and will stop a person from being able to continue to run.
- However, speed training increases the muscles tolerance to lactic acid, so a person can sprint for longer at a higher intensity before they experience fatigue.

See page 51 for more on speed training.

You may have experienced the effect of lactic acid build-up with muscles feeling sore at the end of a sprint or longer race.

Now try this

Explain why muscular endurance training is needed for long-distance cycling races.

Muscle endurance is the ability of a muscle or muscle group to keep contracting for long periods of time.

The effects of long-term fitness training: muscular strength and power training

Taking part in strength training and power training will mainly result in adaptations to the muscular and skeletal body systems, including muscle hypertrophy, increased tendon and ligament strength and increased bone density.

Muscle hypertrophy

Strength training produces micro tears in the muscle fibres that are exercised. The body responds by repairing these fibres so that they become bigger. This process is called **hypertrophy**.

Bigger muscle fibres make those muscles stronger, as the more muscle tissue a person has the more force they can generate.

Increased tendon and ligament strength

Tendons join muscle to bone and ligaments join bones to bones. Strength and power training will increase the strength of these tissues. This occurs from increasing the collagen levels in both types of tissue, which has the effect of increasing their strength. This means they can withstand higher forces before they tear so this adaptation is helpful for a sports performer to avoid injuries to these tissues.

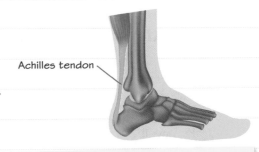

Achilles tendon

The largest and strongest tendon in the body is the Achilles tendon. Weighted squats is a type of training that would increase the strength of the Achilles tendon.

Increased bone density

- Our bones need to contain specific minerals to increase the density and make them stronger. This helps to reduce the risk of a person fracturing their bone when they take part in sport, such as if they fall to the ground when being tackled in rugby.
- Our skeleton is continually repairing and rebuilding (a process called remodelling).
- Strength training and power training both have the effect of stimulating the lay down of minerals in bone tissue, which helps to keep them strong.

The image on the left shows normal bone density. The image on the right shows low bone density.

Now try this

Alex is a basketball player.

Explain why taking part in free-weight training will increase his strength.

Personal information to aid fitness programme design

A fitness programme should be appropriate for the person who will be using it. You need to know the essential information that a fitness programme should include, and how to tailor the programme for the needs of the individual.

1. Personal information
2. Aims
3. Objectives

Information needed for a fitness programme

4. Appropriate components of fitness and method of training
5. Lifestyle and physical activity history
6. Attitudes, the mind and personal motivation for training

Using a person-centred approach

Using a person-centred approach means finding out more about the participant and using their personal information to help design the training programme. Personal information you need to gather includes:

- the participant's current state of health
- the activities they like and dislike
- their availability for exercise.

Using questionnaires to gather personal information

A **PAR-Q** is a type of health-screening questionnaire used to assess a person's medical history.

- It is designed to discover any risk factors that may make physical activity inadvisable.
- All the questions have yes/no answer choices. If the person answers 'yes' to any question, they should consult a doctor before taking part in physical activity.

A **lifestyle questionnaire** is used to gain an overview of how the participant's lifestyle might impact on the design of a fitness programme.

A lifestyle questionnaire should include questions on:

- current activity levels
- drinking alcohol
- stress levels
- diet
- smoking
- sleep.

If you answer yes, to any questions, please give details below.

Question	Yes	No
1 Has your doctor ever told you that you have a heart condition?	☐	☐

Example of a question on a health-screening questionnaire

Confidentiality

Any information you take from a participant must be kept confidential, in line with the latest Data Protection Act. This means that the information should be stored securely so that no unauthorised person can gain access to it.

Setting aims and objectives

Aims: The overall aim of a fitness programme is what the participant hopes to be able to achieve. Some common aims are to:

- improve sporting performance
- lose excess body fat
- be fit enough to take part in an endurance event
- build muscle or to increase strength.

Objectives: these are all the things the participant needs to do in order to achieve their main aim, for example:

- Take part in four swimming training sessions per week, two of which will be in open water.

Now try this

Explain why a PAR-Q should be completed before a participant takes part in sport or physical activity.

Remember that PAR-Q stands for Physical Activity Readiness Questionnaire.

Fitness programme design

The information you have gathered from the participant (revised on page 60) will help you to build a safe fitness programme to help them achieve their fitness aims and objectives.

Choosing appropriate components of fitness

The training programme should target one or more of the components of fitness:

- aerobic endurance
- muscular endurance
- flexibility
- speed
- strength
- power.

The components of fitness that are important for the participant will be determined by their sport or activity and the participant's main aim (revised on page 60).

- Results from fitness tests will highlight which components of fitness need to be improved.
- It is also important to incorporate training to maintain high levels of fitness in components where the participant is already strong.

> Revise the components of fitness on page 1 and fitness tests on pages 20–44.

> Where possible, try to find ways to incorporate fitness training into the participant's everyday lifestyle, for example running or cycling to work.

Fitness programme design using the FITT principles and additional principles of training

When designing the fitness programme, you need to include:

- frequency – number of times per week to train
- intensity of training
- time spent training
- types of training and exercises
- rest days
- training specific to the needs of the sport or fitness goal
- individual differences to meet the needs of the individual
- adaptation to update the training programme based on the adaptation to training by the individual
- reversibility ensuring the person does not need to stop training so that their fitness gains are not lost.

> Revise training methods for each component of fitness on pages 47–54.

Safe design

To make sure that the fitness programme is safe for the participant, the exercises must be at the right level for their current fitness. This will include:

- setting exercises at the right level of intensity
- selecting appropriate training methods.

For example, it might be safer for a person who is new to weight training to use fixed resistance machines rather than free weights, as there is less chance of injury from performing the lift incorrectly or dropping the weight.

Involving the participant

It is vital that the participant is involved in the programme design. You should consult the participant on:

☑ setting the aims and objectives – this will motivate the participant to take part in and persevere with the fitness programme

☑ deciding which days they will train on and for how long – based on their availability

☑ selecting the types of exercises – to ensure that they are enjoyable.

Now try this

Alex plays for a club rugby team. His fitness test results show that he needs to improve his strength.

1 State **one** training method that could be included in Alex's fitness programme to improve his strength.

2 Explain **two** ways in which Alex's coach can ensure that the fitness programme is safe for Alex to use.

Motivational techniques for fitness programming

Motivation can be defined as the internal mechanisms and external stimuli that arouse and direct behaviour. In other words, what drives people to behave in a particular way. We can be motivated to participate in sport or activity in many different ways.

Sports psychology and motivation

- **Psychology** is the study of the mind and how it affects behaviours.
- **Sport psychology** is the study of how the mind affects actions and performance when taking part in sport and activity.
- Sports psychologists study **motivation** because they want to understand what drives a person to want to continue participating and competing in their sport or activity.

Types of motivation

There are two types of motivation:

1 Intrinsic motivation

A person is motivated by internal factors, not external rewards. The motivation to do something comes from how that action makes the person feel.

Examples of intrinsic motivation for taking part in sport or activity include:

- enjoyment of the sport or activity itself
- enjoyment from being with others in a sports club or team
- the challenge of progressing in the sport or activity
- the feeling of becoming fitter
- pride from attaining higher levels of achievement.

2 Extrinsic motivation

A person is motivated by external rewards for taking part or for doing well. The rewards can be tangible or intangible.

- **Tangible rewards** are physical rewards, such as money, a prize or a trophy.
- **Intangible rewards** are non-physical rewards, such as praise or recognition.

Examples of extrinsic motivation for taking part in sport or activity include:

- entering a competition because prize money is on offer
- praise from sports leaders, family members and friends
- public recognition for succeeding in a sport or event.

Intrinsic and extrinsic motivation

Many sportspeople are motivated by a combination of both intrinsic and extrinsic motivation.

☑ They want to perform well in an event because they gain feelings of pride as well as the adrenalin rush of competing.

☑ At the same time, they want to gain the recognition or prize that comes from winning.

Children might take part in a sports day race because they hope to win tangible rewards such as a medal.

Now try this

Nathan takes part in weekly five-a-side football games because he enjoys playing the game.

1 Identify the type of motivation that makes Nathan participate in the five-a-side football games.
2 Describe what is meant by a tangible reward.

Goal setting

A **goal** is what a sports performer is aiming to achieve. Goal setting can help increase and direct motivation to help a performer to continue to train, in order to improve an aspect or a number of areas of their sporting performance.

Personal goals

A person can set their own goals or they could work with a coach or fitness professional to help set their goals. Goals should be **SMARTER**:

Specific – the goal must be specific to what you want to achieve, e.g. I want to improve upper body strength.

Measurable – goals must be stated in a way that is measurable, e.g. I want to increase my chest press one rep max to 100 kg.

Achievable – the person has to have access to the training and the time to take part in it in order to meet the goal.

Realistic – it must be possible to actually reach this goal and not expect improvements beyond what can be achieved in the time frames and current fitness or ability level of the person setting the goals.

SMARTER

Recorded – the results should be written down so that the performer can see how close they are to achieving their goal and how long it takes to reach it.

Exciting – the goal should be something the person really wants to achieve and have an impact on their sports performance, in order for them to be motivated to attend regular training and work hard while training to try and achieve the goal.

Time – there must be a set timescale or deadline on the goal. This means you can review your success. It is best to put a date you wish to achieve the goal by.

Short-term goals

Short-term goals are set over a brief period of time, usually from one day to one month. A short-term goal may relate to what you want to achieve in one training session or where you want to be by the end of the month.

Usually short-term goals are set to help work up to long-term goals. It is important to set both short-term and long-term goals, particularly short-term goals because they will give a person more motivation to act now.

Long-term goals

Long-term goals will run from three months to over several years. You may even set some lifetime goals that run until you retire from your sport. In sport we set long-term goals to cover a season or a sporting year. The period between one and three months would be called medium-term goals.

Influence of goal setting on motivation

Provide direction for behaviour

Goal setting helps to provide performers with a focus so that they can concentrate on achieving that goal. This can help them to avoid taking part in activities that may detract from achieving the goal.

Maintains focus on the task in hand

When a goal has been set and the performer is able to monitor and see their progress in coming closer to achieving the goal, it helps them to appreciate that the training programme is working. This will help them to put in more effort and ensure they attend each training session to help them to continue to improve and come closer to reaching their goal.

Now try this

Why would the SMARTER principle 'time' increase Katie's motivation to train?

Benefits of motivation for the sports performer

Increasing a participant's motivation has a positive effect on their performance in a sport or activity.

Maintenance of intensity

Maintenance of training and increased participation by continuing to take part in regular sport/fitness activities

Benefits of increased motivation

Increased fitness

Improved performance

Intrinsic and extrinsic rewards

① Maintenance of intensity

- A highly motivated person is able to push themselves harder and exercise at a higher intensity than a person with lower motivation levels.
- In training, a highly motivated person might be able to shut out feelings of fatigue and pain and work at maximum capacity during each training session.
- They are able to use their mind to drive them on to succeed.

② Maintenance of training and increased participation

- For health and fitness gains, participation in sport and activity should take place regularly each week.
- With work, study and other commitments, it can be difficult for people to fit training into a busy schedule.
- If someone's motivation levels are high enough and are maintained, this will help them to overcome reluctance to take part in training, and continue to participate on a regular basis.

③ Increased fitness

High motivation levels will help a person to stick to their training programme, so that they continue to get up early or dedicate time to training, which will increase their fitness levels.

④ Improved performance

- High levels of motivation fitness will help a person to improve their sporting performance such as being able to run faster from speed training or being able to jump higher from plyometric training.
- If they are motivated, a person's fitness levels and skills will improve through regular training, and they will be able to compete at a higher level.
- For a basketball player, this would allow them to be able to dribble more quickly with the ball and then be able to jump high to perform a lay up, both of which will give the opportunity to score more baskets and therefore increase their sporting performance.

⑤ Increased intrinsic and extrinsic rewards

- Regular participation in sport and training brings increased intrinsic rewards. The participant will continue to enjoy the positive feelings they get from their sport or activity.
- In addition, they are more likely to benefit from extrinsic rewards as their fitness and skills improve, and they may succeed in competition.

Revise examples of intrinsic and extrinsic motivation on page 62.

Enjoying training sessions significantly increases motivation.

Now try this

A cricket coach uses a range of methods to increase the motivation levels of his team.

Suggest **two** benefits that the team might experience as a result of increased motivation.

Your Component 3 exam

Your Component 3 exam will be set by Pearson and could cover any of the essential content in the unit. You can revise the unit content in this Revision Guide. This skills section is designed to **revise skills** that might be needed in your exam. The section uses selected content and outcomes to provide examples of ways of applying your skills.

Exam checklist

Before your exam, make sure you:

- ✓ have a black pen that you like and at least one spare
- ✓ have a calculator and put in a new battery if your school does not provide one
- ✓ have double-checked the time and date of your exam
- ✓ get a good night's sleep.

Check the Pearson website

The questions and sample response extracts in this section are provided to help you to revise content and skills.

Ask your tutor or check the Pearson website for the latest **Sample Assessment Material** and **Mark Scheme**, so that you know the structure of the paper and what you need to do. The details of the actual exam may change, so always make sure you are up to date.

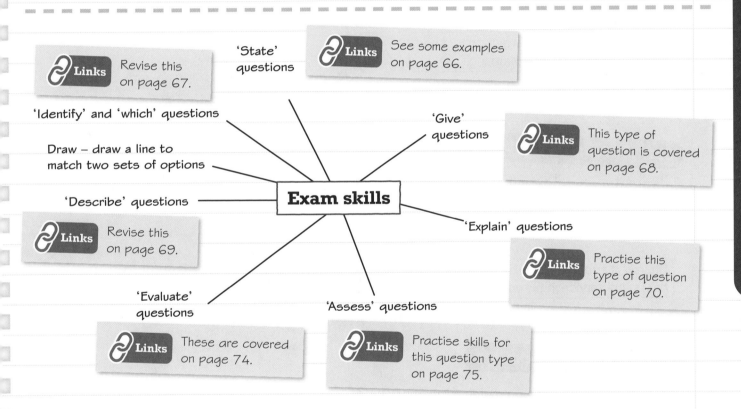

🔗 **Links**   Revise this on page 67.

'State' questions

🔗 **Links**   See some examples on page 66.

'Identify' and 'which' questions

Draw – draw a line to match two sets of options

'Describe' questions

'Give' questions

🔗 **Links**   This type of question is covered on page 68.

Exam skills

🔗 **Links**   Revise this on page 69.

'Explain' questions

🔗 **Links**   Practise this type of question on page 70.

'Evaluate' questions

'Assess' questions

🔗 **Links**   These are covered on page 74.

🔗 **Links**   Practise skills for this question type on page 75.

Now try this

Visit the Pearson website and find the page containing the course materials for BTEC Tech Award in Sport. Look at the latest Component 3 Sample Assessment Material (SAM) for an indication of:

- whether the paper is in parts
- how much time is allowed
- how many marks are allocated
- what types of questions appear on the paper.

Your teacher may already have provided you with a copy of the Sample Assessment Material. You can use this as a 'mock' exam to practise before taking your actual exam.

'State' questions

When responding to a 'state' question, you need to give a definition or an example. This type of question is testing your knowledge of the specification essential content. You should be able to recall the answer.

Izzy is a gymnast. She takes part in some fitness tests.

Complete the table by stating:

i)   The component of fitness tested

ii) Why it would be a suitable test for a gymnast

(4)

Fitness test	Component of fitness	Why it is suitable
Vertical jump test	*Power*	A gymnast needs power when performing a handspring
Stork-stand test	*Static balance*	A gymnast needs balance for beam work

Links Revise the vertical jump test on page 41 and the stork stand test on page 37.

Check what sport is being referred to in the question as some questions will need responses that are appropriate to the person's sport.

Double-check your answer to make sure you have filled in the boxes correctly.

Anita is a triathlete. She wants to test her aerobic endurance for swimming.

State a valid fitness test to test her aerobic endurance for swimming.   **(1)**

Always read the introduction text to each question. This sets the scene and may provide important information.

Sample response extract

12-minute Cooper swim test

Keep your answers to 'state' questions simple. There is no need to give any explanation.

Sharon is a football fitness coach and offers this service in the voluntary sector.

State what is meant by voluntary provision.   (1)

Links Revise provision for taking part in fitness training methods on page 55.

Some 'state' questions might ask you to give a meaning or definition.

Sample response extract

This is where the people providing the service do not charge any money for their time.

Be careful when you are asked to give a meaning. Ensure that your answer provides a brief overview of the focus of the question.

Now try this

Tristan takes part in cross-country running, which requires high levels of aerobic endurance.

State **two** methods of training that would help to improve Tristan's aerobic endurance.   (2)

Method of training 1 ....

Method of training 2 ....

Choose two of the types of aerobic endurance training you have learned about.

 Links You can revise training for aerobic endurance on page 47.

'Identify' and 'which' questions

The command verb 'identify' means that you need to assess factual information given in the question. It is usually enough to answer using one word or sometimes a few words, depending on the information given. The command word 'which' means that you need to identify the correct answer from a list or piece of information or match two things such as definitions to images.

Jack is 17 years old and took part in the sit and reach test. His result was **13 cm**.

Rating	Males (cm)	Females (cm)
Excellent	25+	20+
Very good	17	17
Good	15	16
Average	14	15
Poor	13	14
Very poor	9	10

Table 1

(a) Using **Table 1**, identify the category Jack is in for the sit and reach test. (1)

You could quickly highlight or underline information in the question text and table that might be relevant.

You might be asked to identify information that is presented in a table or chart.

Links Find out more about the sit and reach test on page 26.

In this question you can deduce that Jack is male. You are also told Jack's age, but age is not relevant for the sit and reach test.

Sample response extract

Poor

As the question just asks you to identify the category and there is only one mark, a one-word response is enough.

(b) Which one of the following is **not** a component of the FITT principle?
☐ Frequency
☐ Intrinsic
☐ Time
☐ Type (1)

Links You can revise the FITT principles on page 2.

Go through each of the options in turn and rule out any that you know are definitely components of the FITT principle (as you have been asked which is **not** a component of FITT).

Sample response extract

☐ Frequency
☑ **Intrinsic**
☐ Time
☐ Type

You just need to tick the correct box in your answer.

Now try this

Draw a line to identify the correct fitness test.

 One-minute press-up

 Timed plank test

You will need to recall these tests from your knowledge of the essential content.

Links You can revise the fitness tests on pages 20–44.

'Give' questions

Questions with the command word 'give' might ask you to provide examples, definitions, justifications or reasons. You might need to write one word, a few words or a whole sentence, depending on the information required.

> Michael plays tennis. Before a tennis competition, Michael is highly motivated to play as well as possible in each match.
>
> (a) Give the definition of motivation. (1)

There is often more than one correct way of stating a definition. Here are other correct definitions:
- 'The internal and external factors that make people behave in a particular way'
- 'The reasons why we want to participate in sport or activity'.

Sample response extract

Motivation is the internal mechanism and external stimuli that direct behaviour.

> (b) Give **one** example of how Michael's high level of motivation could benefit him in the tennis competition. (1)

Questions that ask for examples will state how many examples you should give.

Sample response extract

Michael's motivation is likely to make him try harder in the competition.

This answer is clear and to the point, and it contains all the relevant information.

 Links You can revise motivation on page 62.

> Tahani is a sprinter who wants to increase her speed.

 Links You can revise speed training on page 51.

> (c) Give **two** training methods that could be used to improve speed. (2)

There are quite a few different types of training methods for speed, but you need to use the correct terminology to gain credit – increasing speed sprints is not clear; using ropes is also too vague as the type of rope used is important for speed training.

Sample response extract

1. Increasing speed sprints
2. Using ropes

This is a good response as acceleration sprints are a type of speed training.

Improved response extract

1. Acceleration sprints
2. Using bungee ropes

This is another good answer, as bungee ropes allow stretch, which is required for sprint training when working with a partner.

Now try this

> Brian takes part in marathon running events. He takes part in a nine-month continuous training programme to prepare for the marathon run.
>
> Give **one** reason why continuous training is important to prepare for a marathon running event. (1)

 Links You can revise aerobic endurance training on page 47.

Had a look ☐　　Nearly there ☐　　Nailed it! ☐

'Describe' questions

Questions with the command verb 'describe' might ask you to give details about a key concept from the essential content, or to provide an account of a process.

Haniya is training to take part in a 5 km cross-country run. She includes continuous training in her training programme to help prepare for the event.

(a) Describe what is meant by continuous training. (2)

 Links You can revise continuous training on page 47.

You will usually need to write one or two sentences for a 'describe' question in order to provide enough detail.

Sample response extract

Continuous training is where a person exercises at a constant pace for a period of at least 30 minutes.

This response includes good details about continuous training, including what is involved and how long it should last for.

Sheldon takes part in hurdling. To help improve his performance, he carries out static active stretching so that he is able to get into the right position to cross the hurdle quickly.

(b) Describe how to carry out static active stretching. (3)

 Links You can revise static active stretching and other types of flexibility training on page 48.

Sample response extract

To carry out a static active stretch, you need to get your body into the correct position and stretch.

This response is a good start to answering the question, but it needs to give more details about the process involved.

Improved response extract

Get the body into the correct position to stretch the targeted muscle or muscle group, and hold the position for 12–30 seconds. It is done using your own body.

This response gives a complete answer to the question:

- It describes the process involved in doing a static active stretch.
- It includes relevant details, including what you need to do and how long for.

Now try this

Katya's personal trainer has used the principles of training to design a training programme for her. Progressive overload is one of the principles of training.

Describe what is meant by progressive overload. (3)

 Links You can revise progressive overload on page 8.

'Explain' questions

The command verb 'explain' might ask you to make a statement and justify it, or to name an example and give a reason why it is important or relevant.

> Sanjit runs weekly after-school sports sessions at a local primary school. He would like to increase the children's motivation so that they try to focus more on the session.

 Always read the text that sets the scene for the question. It will help you to understand the situation.

(a) Explain **one** type of motivation Sanjit could use to help to increase the children's motivation in his sessions. (2)

Sample response extract

> Sanjit could use extrinsic motivation, which means providing rewards for taking part or for doing well.

This response starts well by naming a type of motivation. However, instead of **describing** what extrinsic motivation is, this learner should **explain** why it is appropriate.

Improved response extract

> Sanjit could use extrinsic motivation because children usually respond well to this type of motivation, in the form of rewards such as certificates or stickers.

This is a better response because it names one of the two types of motivation, and gives a good reason why this would be appropriate for Sanjit to use for motivating children.

Answers to 'explain' questions often contain the words 'because' or 'so'.

 Links You can revise the two types of motivation (intrinsic and extrinsic) on page 62.

> Hannah makes sure that she completes a full warm-up before taking part in the sit and reach fitness test.

 Links You can revise the sit and reach test on page 26.

Explain **one** reason why it is important for Hannah to be fully warmed-up before taking part in the sit and reach test. (2)

Sample response extract

> It is important so that her muscles are fully warmed up.

This response states one reason why warming up is important. However, the question requires one reason **and** an explanation of **why** it is important.

Improved response extract

> It is important so that her muscles can be fully warmed-up as they become more pliable when they are warm, which will allow her to stretch further in the sit and reach test.

This response gives a complete answer:
- It gives one relevant reason.
- It explains why that reason is important.

Start by stating what component of fitness fartlek training improves then give the benefits of this for cross country running performance.

Now try this

> Penny is a cross-country runner. Her coach has advised her to take part in fartlek training to improve her cross-country running performance.

Explain why fartlek training may help Penny's cross-country running performance. (2)

 Links You can revise fartlek training on page 47.

Planning your responses to longer-answer questions

Some questions in your Component 3 exam will require longer answers. The command verbs for these questions include 'discuss', 'evaluate' and 'assess'. Revise these question types on pages 73–75.

Allow yourself some time to plan your answers to longer-answer questions, to make sure you can structure them well and don't leave anything important out.

Daphne is a long-distance swimmer. She is training for a 3 km open-water swim which will take place in six weeks' time.

Table 1 shows Daphne's weekly training programme.

Day	Training
Mon	60 minutes continuous training – swimming lengths of pool
Tues	60 minutes circuit training – land-based using low weights
Wed	30 minutes sprint training – sprint swims in the pool
Thu	60 minutes continuous training – swimming lengths of the pool
Fri	60 minutes free weight training – land-based using heavy weights
Sat	60 minutes continuous training – swimming lengths of the pool
Sun	30 minutes sprint training – sprint swims in the pool

Table 1

Discuss the suitability of Daphne's training programme to prepare her for the 3 km open-water swim. **(6)**

Points to remember for longer-answer questions

✓ Refer to all the information provided, including any tables

✓ Consider all the different aspects of the situation, such as the positives and negatives

✓ Show your knowledge and understanding of the Component 3 content

✓ Only include information that is relevant to the question being asked

✓ Use key terms correctly

✓ Make links between different pieces of information

✓ You might need to draw conclusions or make recommendations based on all the points you have made.

The key word in this question is 'discuss'. You will need to explore in detail how well the training programme will help prepare Daphne for the event.

Sample notes extract

<u>Positives:</u>

- Continuous training (20 min+) → aerobic endurance: 3 km swim = aerobic event

- Circuit training low weights → muscular endurance: 3 km swim = repeated muscle contractions.

<u>Negatives:</u>

- Free weight training heavy weights → muscular strength: not necessary

- Sprint training → increased speed: not necessary

- 0 rest days → overtraining/injury.

Organising your notes under headings will help you to structure your answer into paragraphs.

These notes clearly identify the positives and negatives of Daphne's training programme.

Make sure you show your understanding of the key concepts. These notes make links between each type of training and the component of fitness it is designed to improve.

The sample notes continue on the next page.

Planning your responses to longer-answer questions (continued)

The example notes extract starts on page 71 and continues below.

Summary:

- Well-planned programme
- Strength and speed training not necessary
- Add rest days to allow recovery and adaptations to training
- One more continuous training session – more aerobic endurance.

You won't have much time to plan in the exam, so your plan doesn't need to be as detailed as this one. You could:

- write a quick list of key words
- annotate the question and table instead
- use abbreviations, but make sure that you understand them.

 Links Revise the principles of specificity and overtraining on pages 7 and 11.

 Links Revise training for the different components of fitness on pages 47–54.

Now try this

Write a **brief plan** to help you answer the 'discuss' question below. (You will be writing a full answer to this question on page 73.)

> Tom is training for a 10 km cross-country race which is due to take place in six weeks.

Table 2 shows his training programme.

Day	Training	Intensity (% Max HR)
Mon	Circuit training	60%
Tues	Continuous training	70%
Wed	Anaerobic hill sprints	70%
Thurs	Continuous training	60%
Fri	Continuous training	70%
Sat	Circuit training	60%
Sun	Rest	

Table 2

Discuss the suitability of Tom's training to develop his cross-country running performance.

(6)

Consider each type of training in turn. Which component of fitness does it develop? Is this appropriate for Tom's event?

Look at **all** the information you are given. Is the intensity appropriate for each training method?

Are there any other aspects of the programme that you need to discuss (such as the rest day)? Is there anything missing (such as time or progressive overload)?

 Links You will need to bring together knowledge from different parts of Component 3:

- training for different components of fitness (pages 47–53)
- FITT principles and principles of training, particularly intensity (page 4) and training zones (page 13).

In your plan list the positives of the training programme, the negatives and the points you should include in your summary.

'Discuss' questions

When answering 'discuss' questions, make sure you consider all the different aspects of the situation you are given. Look back at the question and table on page 71, and the learner's plan for a response. Then read the learner's completed response below. The annotations will help you understand what makes this response effective.

Sample response extract

Continuous training will improve Daphne's aerobic endurance, which is necessary to be able to swim 3 km as this is an aerobic event. Continuous training needs to last at least 20 minutes to develop aerobic endurance. Daphne spends twice as long as this minimum time, which will help develop her aerobic endurance.

 Make links between the information given in the question and your knowledge of the issues. One of the links made in this answer is the relevance of continuous training for the 3 km swim event.

Circuit training will develop Daphne's muscular endurance as she uses low weights. Her muscles will have to keep contracting for long periods of time to keep swimming for 3 km, so training for muscular endurance is beneficial for her event.

 A well-developed discussion will consider the different aspects of the question. In this case, the learner explores both the positives and negatives of Daphne's programme.

However, she doesn't have a rest day, which is very important to help prevent overtraining and reduce the risk of injury.

 Show accurate knowledge and understanding of the essential content. This answer shows understanding of overtraining and of the purposes of strength training and sprint training.

Training sessions that aim to develop muscular strength using heavy free weights, and sprint training to develop speed are not very important for a 3 km long-distance swim.

 Make sure your discussion is clear and logical. This answer considers each of the main aspects of the programme in turn. It doesn't jump about between issues.

Continuous training and circuit training are both good for improving the aerobic and muscular endurance that Daphne needs. Daphne doesn't need the free weight and sprint sessions. Instead, she should have one or two rest days to allow her body time to recover and to adapt to the training sessions already completed.

 This learner has finished by summarising the key points they have made in their answer.

 See also the tips for longer answer questions on pages 71 and 72.

Now try this

Look at the 'discuss' question at the bottom of page 72 and the plan that you wrote for this question.

Use your plan to write a full answer to the 'now try this' question on page 72.

 Look back at the tips for longer-answer questions on page 71.

'Evaluate' questions

When answering 'evaluate' questions, you need to consider both sides of a given situation or compare two options. You will need to examine the strengths and weaknesses or advantages and disadvantages, and finish by making a judgement. Remind yourself of the tips for longer-answer questions on pages 71–72.

> Andy takes part in the Harvard step test. He uses the following technology to complete the test:
> - a heart rate monitor to measure his heart rate
> - appropriate footwear.
>
> Evaluate the use of this technology when carrying out the Harvard step test. (6)

Always read the scenario text carefully.

 Links You can revise the Harvard step test on page 21.

Here, you need to give the pros and cons of using technology and appropriate footwear to complete the Harvard step test and finish with a judgement about which will benefit Andy the most.

Sample response extract

The Harvard Step test involves stepping on and off a bench for a period of time, and testing the person's ability to recover from strenuous exercise. The participant's pulse must be measured at the correct time (1–1.5 minutes, 2–2.5 minutes and 3–3.5 minutes after finishing).

The benefit of using a heart rate monitor rather than measuring his own pulse is that the heart rate results will be more accurate, which will increase the reliability of the test.

The footwear could help to improve his grip on the floor and bench, which will help to stop him slipping when taking part in the test. This will ensure he is stepping at the right pace, which will increase the reliability of the test.

However, the heart rate monitor is expensive, so it is not available for everyone to use.

Sports footwear can be expensive so is not available for everyone to use. However, the participant should ensure they wear the same, comfortable footwear each time to make sure the test is reliable.

Overall, the use of this technology can lead to improved reliability and fitness test scores, giving a more accurate reflection of the individual's ability.

This answer starts well by making links between the technology and the fitness test.

Always give the negatives as well as the positives for each option.

Make sure your answer is relevant. Here the learner relates every point they make to the Harvard fitness test.

You will usually need to finish your answer to an 'evaluate' question with a conclusion. This should:
- make a judgement
- give a direct answer to the question
- be supported by evidence from the rest of your answer.

Now try this

> Alicia is 12 years old and is a sprinter. She will be competing in the 100 m at the schools district athletics competition in eight weeks' time. She takes part in speed training to prepare for the athletics competition.
>
> Evaluate **two** training methods Alicia could use to increase her speed. (6)

 **Links** Revise methods to increase speed on page 51.

Remember to include the pros and cons of each method and finish with a conclusion. Which methods do you recommend for Alicia and why?

'Assess' questions

An 'assess' question will usually be based on information provided. You will need to examine and interpret the information in order to answer the question.

> Steve is a basketball player. He takes part in power and speed training to help improve his basketball performance.

Links You can revise speed and power training on pages 51 and 53.

> Assess the importance of high levels of power and speed when taking part in a basketball game. (6)

This question asks you to focus on the two types of training and how they may be used in basketball.

Sample response extract

Power is the product of speed and strength to allow for explosive movements in sport. This could be used in basketball for the player to be able to jump up high to take a shot so that they are closer to the hoop. If they are closer when taking a shot they are more likely to score.

This answer begins with definitions of each component of fitness, then links to how they are used in the selected sport.

Speed is distance divided by time and the time it takes to move the body or a body part quickly in an event or game. A basketball player will need high levels of speed to be able to sprint down the court to make a fast break to be in with a chance of performing a successful lay up, as there would be less opposition at the end of the court if he was able to outsprint them.

Focus on the situation and information you have been given.

Draw on your knowledge from different parts of the essential content and make links between them.

High levels of both power and speed are important for a basketball player, otherwise they would have less chance of being able to jump up high enough or get into the best position on court to score points in a basketball game.

'Assess' questions require a detailed response. Here the learner explains why power and speed are important for Jan's sport.

Make sure your answer includes an assessment of the importance of each component of fitness to basketball performance.

Now try this

Jan is working with her coach to devise a training programme to help to improve her fitness for gymnastics.

An example of the components of fitness to be trained each week is shown in **Table 1**.

Links Revise the four FITT principles on page 2.

Day	Component of fitness to be trained	Training method	Duration of session	Intensity
Mon	Power	Plyometrics	30 min	High
Tue	Flexibility	Static stretching	30 min	Moderate
Wed	Strength	Resistance machines	30 min	High
Thurs	Power	Plyometrics	30 min	High
Fri	Flexibility	Static stretching	30 min	Moderate
Sat	Strength	Resistance machines	30 min	High
Sun	Rest			

Table 1

Organise your answer by writing a paragraph about the two FITT principles: how each has been applied to Jan's training and how each will help to improve her performance.

Assess how the F and the I from the FITT principles are being used to plan Jan's fitness training in order to improve her gymnastics performance. (6)

Answers

1 The importance of fitness for successful participation in sport

c) Muscular endurance and aerobic endurance

2 The basic principles of training: FITT principles

1 Frequency, intensity.
2 Frequency: for example, three times per week.
   Intensity: for example, 60% Max HR; moderate intensity.

3 Frequency

1 Three sessions per week
2 Four times per week – before and after every training session

4 Intensity

1 202 bpm
2 141 bpm
3 It can be used to estimate training zones if a person does not have a heart rate monitor to measure their heart rate.

5 Type

Individual responses could include:
1 Plyometrics
2 Tanya could take part in bouncing exercises where she jumps off a bench onto the ground and straight back up onto another bench. Other types of plyometric training exercises include hopping, lunging, press-ups with a clap, passing a medicine ball to a partner.

6 Time

1 Individual responses could include cycling, jogging, circuit training or any other type of activity used to develop aerobic endurance or muscular endurance.
2 Sean should exercise for at least 28 minutes.

7 Additional principles of training: specificity

Individual responses might vary but could include the following:
- Ryan could take part in rowing on a river to improve his fitness for rowing.
- He could use a rowing machine in a gym.

8 Progressive overload

Progressive overload means gradually increasing the participant's workload over time to achieve an improvement in their fitness.

9 Individual differences

1 Location of training – it is 5 miles away so Jackie will need to take public transport or ask her parents to give her a lift.
2 Cost – cost of tennis equipment and clothing may affect accessibility to training.
3 Commitments – Jackie is still at school so she will have homework to complete, which will affect her availability to train.

10 Rest and recovery and adaptation

A rest day is needed so that the person's body can recover from training. This gives the body time to adapt to the training that has taken place so that fitness levels for that component of fitness can improve.

11 Reversibility

Individual responses might vary. Possible answers include injury or illness that prevents the individual training, or a holiday where there are no training facilities.

12 Variation

Sanjid could change his training location for one session a week. Instead of running on the road he could run on a treadmill in the gym. He could also try running as part of a group rather than on his own.

13 Training zones

1 220 – Sunita's age (22) = 198 bpm
2 For training in the aerobic training zone, Sunita's heart rate should be a minimum of 139 bpm (70%) and a maximum of 158 bpm (80%).

14 Technology to measure exercise intensity

Using technology means the person taking part in exercise does not have to stop their exercise session to measure their heart rate because the technology can provide an instant reading. If they had to measure their heart rate by taking their pulse, they would usually have to stop exercising in order to find their pulse and then measure it.

15 Fitness testing: importance to sports performers and coaches

Baseline scores are important because they provide a score to compare further test scores against, which helps to monitor an individual's performance.

16 Pre-fitness test procedures: screening

A PAR-Q assesses a person's medical history and helps to find out if the person is well enough to take part in exercise safely or whether they need medical clearance first.

17 Pre-fitness test procedures: calibration of equipment and test protocol

Any three from the following; ensure the participant:
- is wearing appropriate clothing
- has not had a heavy meal three hours before the test
- has had a good night's sleep
- has not trained on the day and is fully recovered from previous training
- has avoided stimulants such as tea, coffee or nicotine for two hours before the test.
The PAR-Q will have checked for medical clearance and injuries so these responses cannot be given any credit.

18 Choosing appropriate fitness tests and interpreting results

If a fitness test is selected that is too challenging for a participant it could lead to injury or demotivation.

19 Reliability, validity and practicality of fitness testing

Any three from the following:
- Ensure the participant carries out the same length and type of warm-up.
- The test is carried out at the same time of day.
- Each participant has had a similar amount of sleep compared to when they took the first test.
- The sports hall is at the same temperature.
- The sports hall has the same surface.

- Participants are wearing similar clothing or footwear as the last test.
- All equipment is fully calibrated.
- Participants have the same motivation levels.
- The test is carried out in the same environment.
- The same person administers the test.
- The test procedure is carried out in line with the standardised approach.

20 Fitness tests for aerobic endurance: multi-stage fitness test and Yo-Yo test

Too short a distance will mean the participant will be able to achieve a higher score than they would normally have achieved if the distance had been measured accurately as they will not have to run so far. If the test is taken again with the correct distance measured, the participant will get lower test results compared to the first test but their aerobic fitness levels may remain the same.

21 Fitness tests for aerobic endurance: Harvard step test

$$\frac{30000}{(140 + 128 + 110)}$$

$$= \frac{30000}{378}$$

$$= 79$$

22 Fitness tests for aerobic endurance: 12-minute Cooper test

The test is submaximal, so the person does not have to run to exhaustion and the person taking the test can go at their own pace if they need to. The multi-stage fitness test sets the pace for the person, which may be too fast for them.

23 Fitness tests for muscular endurance: one-minute press-up test

1 The change in fitness test method would affect the reliability of the test results, as the full press-up test is more difficult to complete. This means Anita may complete fewer press-ups in the second test compared to the first.
2 Average

24 Fitness test for muscular endurance: one-minute sit-up test

1 The change in fitness test method would affect the reliability of the test results, as the full press-up test the test more difficult to complete. This means Mina may complete fewer sit-ups in the second test compared to the first.
2 Good

25 Fitness test for muscular endurance: timed plank test

Below average

26 Fitness tests for flexibility: sit and reach test

1 When completing a hurdle, the person has to be able to adopt a position that requires high levels of flexibility in their hamstrings and lower back so that they can jump over the hurdle effectively and efficiently.
2 Above average

27 Fitness tests for flexibility: calf muscle flexibility test

Any sport that requires the person to be able to perform movements that require a large range of movement, e.g. gymnastics, martial arts.

28 Fitness tests for flexibility: shoulder flexibility test

Good

29 Fitness tests for speed: 30 m sprint tests

The field would have a different surface from the sports hall and may have less grip so the person would be able to run faster on the sports hall surface.
A field is outside so the weather may affect running performance, e.g. if it is windy, this would reduce the person's speed compared to when they took the test inside the sports hall.

30 Fitness tests for strength: grip dynamometer test

It tells you that Antoni's grip strength is below average.

31 Fitness test for strength: one rep max test

Good

32 Fitness tests for body composition: body mass index (BMI)

The BMI test is not a valid test for body composition for a sprinter as they will have a high muscle mass and the test does not distinguish between muscle mass and fat mass. As a sprinter has high levels of muscle, the BMI test will show the person as overweight when they may have very little body fat.

33 Fitness tests for body composition: bioelectrical impedance analysis

Exercising before the test
Drinking before the test

34 Fitness tests for body composition: waist-to-hip ratio

1 $\frac{32}{34} = 0.94$

2 Low

35 Fitness test for agility: Illinois agility run test

Above average

36 Fitness tests for agility: T test

1 A tennis player is always facing forwards to see their opponent and has to run from side to side, and forwards and backwards, which is replicated in a T test. The Illinois agility run test, however, involves the person running around cones, which is not something that a tennis player would be doing when they are playing a game of tennis.
2 Average

37 Fitness tests for balance: stork stand test

Venkat would achieve a 'good' rating.

38 Fitness tests for balance: Y balance test

The reach indicators are set out so that they form a Y shape as the person has to move the reach indicators in three different directions following a Y-shape pattern.

39 Fitness tests for coordination: alternate-hand wall-toss test

Sasha would achieve an 'average' rating.

40 Fitness tests for coordination: stick flip coordination test

Not being allowed to take the practice tests would decrease the reliability of the test results as the test requires the person to learn a new technique. When Sam is re-tested he may improve his performance, but this could be because he has a better idea of how to perform the flips rather than his coordination improving.

41 Fitness tests for power: vertical jump test

1   The high jump requires a person to have high levels of power in their legs to be able to jump high over the bar. The vertical jump test measures power in the legs and has a jumping action so is a valid test for a high jumper.
2   Above average

42 Fitness tests for power: standing long/broad jump

The test measures power to jump high rather than power in the arms to throw or hit the ball in baseball. This means it is more sports specific for a netballer when jumping high to defend the net when the opposition are shooting.

43 Fitness tests for power: Margaria-Kalamen power test

To test her power, as Shannon needs to be able to jump over the hurdles quickly to win the 400 m hurdling race.

44 Fitness tests for reaction time: ruler drop test

Average

45 Warm-up

Any two from: pulse raiser, mobiliser, stretch

46 Cool down

A person could decrease their jogging rate so they jog more slowly and gradually start to walk.

47 Fitness training methods for aerobic endurance

A cross-country runner could increase resistance by wearing a weighted back pack. This will increase the weight they have to carry when they are running so will make them work harder.

48 Fitness training methods for flexibility

PNF stretching would be the best method of flexibility training as it increases flexibility at a faster rate compared to other methods of stretching.

49 Fitness training methods for muscular endurance

Anita should use a high number of reps and low weights.

50 Fitness training methods for muscular strength

Fixed resistance machines would be the best form of strength training for Molly because there is less chance of her getting injured using this form of training compared to using free weights.

51 Fitness training methods for speed

Rugby players will usually be moving before they start to sprint so acceleration sprints would be an appropriate method of speed training.
Or:
Rugby players will usually have rest periods in between sprints so interval training would be an appropriate method of speed training.

52 Fitness training methods for agility, coordination and reaction time

A sprint swimmer should start on swimming blocks and have a coach give them the signal to start at irregular timings so that they have to dive in as quickly as possible after they hear this signal.

53 Fitness training methods for power

Barrier hopping would help to improve Keanu's hurdling performance as this is a type of plyometrics training, which will improve power and also focuses on the leg muscles used in the hurdling race.

54 Fitness training methods for balance

Jan could use a balance board while holding a balanced position that she would need to hold while on the beam.

55 Public, private and voluntary provision

Provision	Advantage of type of provision	Benefit to the performer
Private provision	Shazny will have access to the latest training equipment	Increased motivation to attend each training session

56 The effects of long-term fitness training: aerobic endurance training

David's heart will undergo cardiac hypertrophy, which means it will pump out more blood per beat. When David is running he will be able to transport more oxygen and nutrients to the working muscles, which will help him to keep running for longer and at a faster pace.

57 The effects of long-term fitness training: flexibility training

A butterfly swimmer will need high levels of flexibility in the shoulder so that they have a wide range of movement around this joint to perform the arm action required for butterfly stroke.

58 The effects of long-term fitness training: muscular endurance and speed training

Long-distance cycling requires the leg muscles to continue to contract for long periods of time, so they need oxygen and nutrients. Muscular endurance training results in capillarisation around the muscle tissues, which increases the supply of oxygen and nutrients to the working muscles as well as removing waste products.

59 The effects of long-term fitness training: muscular strength and power training

Free-weight training produces micro tears in Alex's muscle fibres. This stimulates the muscle tissue to repair itself and in so doing increases the size of the muscle fibre. The more muscle tissue Alex has, the more force his muscles will be able to produce so his strength will increase.

60 Personal information to aid fitness programme design

A PAR-Q assesses a participant's medical history. It is designed to help the sports/activity leader find out if the participant is well enough to take part in sport or activity, or whether they need medical clearance or advice.

61 Fitness programme design

1   Free weights or resistance machines
2   Individual responses may vary. Answers could include:
- Set the training at the correct level of intensity for Alex, e.g. size of weights used; number of reps and sets.
- Recommend fixed resistance machines rather than free weights if Alex is new to strength training.
- Make sure that Alex knows the correct technique for each exercise, to avoid the risk of injury.

62 Motivational techniques for fitness programming

1   Intrinsic
2   A tangible reward is a physical reward such as prize money or a trophy.

63 Goal setting

Having a set time to complete the goal ensures Katie completes each training session so that she can try and achieve the goal in the time given.

64 Benefits of motivation for the sports performer

Individual responses might vary. Any two from:
- Players will put in a high intensity of effort during participation.
- Players will continue to take part on a regular basis.
- Players will have increased fitness levels.
- Players will have improved performance.

66 'State' questions

Any two from: continuous training, fartlek training, interval training, circuit training.

67 'Identify' and 'which' questions

Timed plank test.

68 'Give' questions

Continuous training is important as it trains aerobic endurance, which is needed to run a marathon event.

69 'Describe' questions

Your description of progressive overload should include the following points:
Gradually increasing the training intensity over a set period of time in order to improve a specific component of fitness. This is necessary to avoid injury and overtraining.

70 'Explain' questions

Your answer should include the following points:
- Fartlek training is used to develop aerobic endurance, which is required to supply oxygen and nutrients to the working muscles so that they can continue to contract for the duration of the race.
- Fartlek training replicates cross-country running as it involves running over different terrain and at different intensities, which Penny will experience when she is running up hills in her race.

71–72 Planning your responses to longer-answer questions

Your plan may include notes on some of the following:
- Circuit training
- Tom needs muscular endurance as his muscles will have to keep contracting for long periods of time to run the full distance of the 10 km race.
- The intensity for circuit training is too low – it should be in the aerobic training zone (70–80% of max HR to develop muscular endurance).
- Anaerobic hill sprints are used to develop power.
- Tom will need power to run at speed up the hills.
- The intensity for anaerobic training is not high enough (it should be at an intensity of 80–100% max HR).

Continuous training develops aerobic endurance.
- This is an aerobic event and this training will allow Tom to keep running at a fast pace for 10 km.
- Continuous training needs to last at least 20 minutes to develop aerobic endurance.
- The intensity of aerobic training is correct (it should be at 70–80% HR max).

Tom's programme includes one rest day.
- This is appropriate as he is training for a big race. It will help prevent overtraining and reduce the risk of injury.

Areas that could be improved:
- The intensity of the circuit training and hill sprint training should be increased to improve Tom's muscular endurance and power.
- The time of each training session should be added to make sure that adaptations will occur.
- The programme should indicate how progressive overload will be achieved.

73 'Discuss' questions

Individual responses will vary, but your answer should develop the points in the plan you made for the previous page (see the answer to pages 71–72 for some suggested points).

74 'Evaluate' questions

Your answer may include some of the following points:
Training methods that can be used to increase speed are interval training and resistance drills.

Interval training
For interval training used to train for speed, work intervals should be short but carried out at a very high intensity followed by a rest or recovery period.

Pros
- Allows Alicia to see whether she is at a similar level of another participant
- Training and improving together will help to increase her confidence

Cons
- Good for sports that have varied intensity with recovery periods, no equipment needed
- No training facility required

Resistance drills
Alicia could use a parachute as this overloads the muscles used for sprinting, which makes them stronger.

Pros
- Good for sports that involve travelling at speed and in a straight line.
- The equipment can be used to add resistance and variety.

Cons
- Equipment can be expensive.
- Only useful for sports that include sprinting in one direction.

Conclusion
Resistance drills would be most appropriate as Alicia's race requires her to run as fast as possible for 100 m with no breaks and in a straight line, which exactly replicates resistance drills. Interval training includes rest periods, which are not permitted in the 100 m sprint race.

75 'Assess' questions

Your answer may include some of the following points:

Frequency

- Jan trains six times a week, which is sufficient to result in fitness gains. This is necessary as it provides sufficient progressive overload to develop the components of fitness required to improve Jan's gymnastics performance.
- She also has a rest day, which is important to allow her body to recover and adapt to the training, which will help her to avoid overtraining and injury.

Intensity

- Intensity is how hard a person trains.
- It is important to work at the right intensity to train for both aerobic and anaerobic fitness.
- Jan will train at high intensity for power and strength. These are both anaerobic activities and so should be carried out at high intensity to increase anaerobic fitness.
- For flexibility training, intensity can be based on a scale of low/moderate/high. There is no specific heart rate or training zone in order to gain fitness adaptations for flexibility training.